T0247676

A Diverse and Trusted Workforce

Examining Elements That Could Contribute to
the Potential for Bias and Sources of Inequity in
National Security Personnel Vetting

SINA BEAGHLEY, JESSICA WELBURN PAIGE, DAVID STEBBINS,
SARAH ZELAZNY, SAMANTHA RYAN, AMY BURNETT CROSS

Prepared for the Performance Accountability Council Program
Management Office
Approved for public release; distribution is unlimited

NATIONAL DEFENSE RESEARCH INSTITUTE

About This Report

Applicants for national security positions are required to provide detailed and personal information as part of the background investigation process to adjudicate their eligibility for a security clearance. As a result, during the course of the personnel vetting process, an individual's race or ethnicity, gender, gender identity, sexual orientation, or neurodivergence (*neurodiversity* being the diversity of all cognitive functions) may be knowable or inferred by the personnel conducting the investigations and adjudications. This study explored the potential for related bias or sources of inequity within the federal personnel vetting process. Such potential biases and inequities could inhibit the U.S. government's goals and abilities to hire national security personnel with diverse backgrounds and varied perspectives.

The research reported here was completed in November 2022 and underwent security review with the sponsor and the Defense Office of Prepublication and Security Review before public release.

RAND National Security Research Division

This research was sponsored by the Security, Suitability, and Credentialing (SSC) Performance Accountability Council Program Management Office (PAC PMO) and conducted within the Forces and Resources Policy Center of the RAND National Security Research Division (NSRD), which operates the National Defense Research Institute (NDRI), a federally funded research and development center sponsored by the Office of the Secretary of Defense, the Joint Staff, the Unified Combatant Commands, the Navy, the Marine Corps, the defense agencies, and the defense intelligence enterprise.

For more information on the RAND Personnel, Readiness, and Health, see www.rand.org/nsrd/prh or contact the director (contact information is provided on the webpage).

Acknowledgments

This study would not have been possible without the support and contributions from several individuals. We thank the PAC PMO sponsors—specifically, David Colangelo, Travis Furman, Heather Clawson, and Renee Oberlin—for their support of this research, responsiveness in assisting with information queries, and helpful feedback. Additionally, we are grateful to our discussion participants for their time, candor, and engagement on this important topic.

We are also appreciative of the support and contributions from several RAND Corporation colleagues. We are grateful to Betsy Hammes from RAND's Knowledge Services staff, who supported our literature review. We also want to thank Molly McIntosh and Daniel Ginsberg in RAND's Personnel, Readiness, and Health program for their leadership, guidance and support of this project.

Finally, we express our gratitude to our peer reviewers—RAND colleagues Marek Posard and Charles Sowell—for their helpful and thoughtful review of this report.

Summary

Issue

Applicants for national security positions are required to provide detailed and personal information as part of the background investigation process to adjudicate their eligibility for a security clearance. As a result, during the course of the personnel vetting process, an individual's race or ethnicity, gender, gender identity, sexual orientation, or neurodivergence (*neurodiversity* being the diversity of all cognitive functions) may be knowable or inferred by the personnel conducting the investigations and adjudications. This study explored the potential for bias or sources of inequity within the federal personnel vetting process. Such potential biases and inequities could inhibit the U.S. government's goals and abilities to hire national security personnel with diverse backgrounds and varied perspectives.

Purpose

The Security, Suitability and Credentialing (SSC) Performance Accountability Council Program Management Office (PAC PMO) sponsored the RAND Corporation's National Defense Research Institute (NDRI) to conduct a study to explore the potential for bias and sources of inequity related to race or ethnicity, gender, gender identity, sexual orientation, or neurodivergence within the personnel vetting process. To that end, we sought to (1) review theories, practices, and studies within the social sciences literature related to race or ethnicity, gender, gender identity, sexual orientation, or neurodiversity biases and sources of inequity, (2) examine elements of the security clearance personnel vetting process in the context of such potential biases or inequities, and (3) provide related recommendations for personnel vetting policymakers.

Approach

We conducted this study using a two-pronged research approach consisting of reviews of relevant literature and discussions with personnel vetting and diversity, equity, inclusion, and accessibility (DEIA) experts about elements in the personnel vetting process that have the potential for bias and sources of inequity. We first considered structural elements of the personnel vetting process, specifically as it relates to the most rigorous version of personnel vetting in determining eligibility for a security clearance, including the Standard Form (SF) 86 (SF-86) questionnaire that candidates and staff are required to fill out and the security clearance adjudicative guidelines. We also considered human elements of the process, including how perceptions and judgments of the investigators, adjudicators, and quality reviewers have the potential to affect the outcome of the process. After analyzing these elements, we developed conclusions, observations, and recommendations for the government to consider related to addressing the potential for biases or inequities in the personnel vetting process.

Conclusions, Observations and Recommendations

Conclusions

There is the potential for bias and sources of inequity in both the structural and human elements of the security clearance personnel vetting process. As part of a personnel vetting investigation, an individual's race or ethnicity, gender, gender identity, sexual orientation, or neurodivergence are either knowable from the documentation they are required to submit as part of the structural element of the process or can be inferred by the personnel conducting the investigative and adjudicative human elements of the process. Human judgment and biases that manifest themselves in other employment or social contexts have the potential to contribute to bias and sources of inequity in the human element of the process of determining security clearance eligibility.

Observations and Recommendations

Observation 1: Some components of the forms and guidelines that make up the structural elements of the security clearance personnel vetting process—including SF-86 (Questionnaire for National Security Positions) and Security Executive Agent Directive 4 (SEAD-4)—have the potential to contribute to bias and sources of inequity because of the nature of the information requested, the language used to request it, and the language contained in the guidelines used to adjudicate that information.

- **Recommendation 1:** Review and revise the SF-86 and SEAD-4 guidelines (and other personnel vetting forms and guidelines) to minimize the potential for bias and sources of inequity related to race or ethnicity, gender, gender identity, sexual orientation, and neurodivergence, while still collecting the information that is essential to support a national security clearance adjudicative decision. Any SF-86 revisions to this end would aim to minimize the possibility of collecting unnecessary revelatory information about individuals that has the significant potential to contribute to bias and sources of inequity in treatment and/or that could result in unintentionally deterring a diverse set of individuals from even applying to national security positions. SEAD-4 guideline review and revisions would (1) evaluate the guidelines themselves to determine whether the overall risk category of the guideline or the language contained in the guideline contribute to the potential of a biased or inequitable adjudication and (2) consider whether new or different mitigation language for the risk factor is required to minimize that potential.

Observation 2: Although training for some personnel vetting staff includes cognitive bias awareness, training for investigators and adjudicators does not include modules that specifically train or prepare personnel vetting staff for engagement with applicants from diverse cultures, experiences, and lifestyles.

- **Recommendation 2:** Implement standardized and tailored training to prepare individuals in the investigative and adjudicative process for interactions with applicants from diverse cultures, experiences, and lifestyles. Such tailored training would be specific to the personnel vetting process, and would include investigator and adjudicator-specific curricula informed by relevant vignettes, real-world case studies, and scenarios. To ensure that there is consistent training across investigative and adjudicative service providers, existing training standards and programs for SSC personnel would need to be revised.

Observation 3: Demographic data related to racial or ethnic, gender, gender identity, sexual orientation, or neurodivergent categories are not collected or analyzed in the context of the security clearance process, limiting the ability to assess the process and adjudicative outcomes for applicants to determine whether and where bias and inequity may be occurring.

- **Recommendation 3:** Explore implementing a mechanism by which personnel vetting applicants could voluntarily and separately provide demographic information about race or ethnicity, gender, gender identity, sexual orientation, or neurodivergence (via a survey or other method) for follow-on analysis that is independent from the formal background investigation and adjudication process. Such data collection would need to include clearly articulated language that defines the purpose of the voluntary data collection; how these data would be used to review personnel vetting files and outcomes in a subsequent analysis; and how this information will be protected and who will and will not have access to it (e.g., it would not be provided to those conducting the background investigation and adjudication). A voluntary data collection effort like this would have limitations based on the number and nature of the submissions, but it could enable an initial effort to analyze whether inequities or disparities may exist in the process—beginning at the application phase, through the investigation and interviews, and ending in adjudication and appeals.

Recent Developments

The formal data collection and analysis that informed this report's conclusions, observations and recommendations occurred between April and November 2022. In the time between the completion of our analysis and the writing of this report, several personnel vetting developments have occurred, including related to recommendations we make above. The federal government now has an effort underway to replace the SFs and questionnaires for personnel vetting with a new proposed Personnel Vetting Questionnaire (PVQ), which seeks to address several bias- and equity-related considerations. [1] Although the government intends to review the SEAD-4 guidelines as part of the overall personnel vetting reform effort, we do not know at this time whether this review will include a review for considering potential for bias and sources of inequity. The government is also in the process of updating its training standards to include objectives and identify principles related to potential for bias and inequity for personnel vetting. These newer efforts are either under development or with implementation still in progress, so an assessment of these related and developing efforts are not included in this report's examination.

---

[1] In Chapter 4 of this report, we provide additional detail about considerations related to potential bias and inequity addressed in the proposed PVQ.

Contents

Figures and Tables

Figures

Tables

CHAPTER 1

Introduction and Background

This chapter provides an overview of the relevant policy background and purpose of this study, details the approach the study team took, and summarizes the report structure. It also provides background related to previous prior RAND research and provides a high-level summary of key components of the personnel vetting process.

Policy Background

During the first years of the Biden administration, officials have advanced diversity, equity, inclusion, and accessibility (DEIA) within the federal workforce as a policy priority, first through Executive Order (EO) 13985—officially titled "Advancing Racial Equity and Support for Underserved Communities Through the Federal Government"—which was issued on President Joseph Biden's first day in office, January 20, 2021. In February 2021, the Biden administration issued National Security Memorandum 3 (NSM-3)—officially titled "Revitalizing America's Foreign Policy and National Security Workforce, Institutions, and Partnerships"—which established an Interagency Working Group on the National Security Workforce and directed it to execute several tasks, including to "assess implementation of security clearance reforms and reciprocity proposals, additional reforms to eliminate bias, and ensure efficient timelines for completion of security clearance investigations" (NSM-3, 2021). Additionally, in a follow-on EO 14035 ("Diversity, Equity, Inclusion, and Accessibility in the Federal Workforce") issued in June 2021, the Director of National Intelligence, in consultation with the Director of the U.S. Office of Personnel Management (OPM) and the heads of other agencies, was instructed to "take steps to mitigate any barriers in security clearance and background investigation processes or LGBTQ+ [lesbian, gay, bisexual, transgender, queer or questioning, and other identities] employees and applicants, in particular transgender and gender non-conforming and non-binary employees and applicants." See Figure 1.1 for a summary of recent EOs and memoranda related to advancing DEIA initiatives within the federal workforce.

Related to personnel vetting specifically, the U.S. government is undertaking a transformational modernization and reform effort referred to as Trusted Workforce 2.0 (TW 2.0) and it is explicitly factoring in principles related to fairness and equity in its implementation. TW 2.0 reforms aim to "better support agencies' missions by reducing the time required to bring new hires onboard, enabling mobility of the Federal workforce, and improving insight into workforce behaviors" (Security, Suitability, and Credentialing Performance Accountabil-

FIGURE 1.1

Recent DEIA Milestones Within the U.S. Government

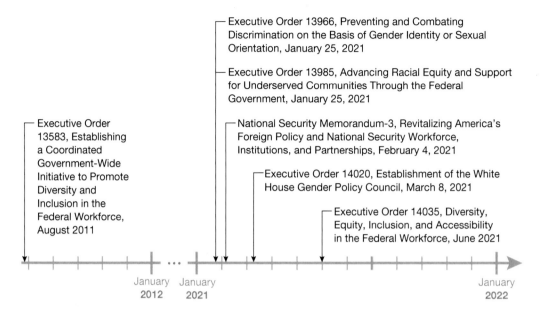

ity Council, 2022, p. 1). [1] The implementation strategy describes how TW 2.0 seeks to modernize information collection from individuals while improving the customer experience and adhering to principles of DEIA.

Purpose

The Security, Suitability and Credentialing (SSC) Performance Accountability Council Program Management Office (PAC PMO) sponsored the RAND Corporation's National Defense Research Institute to conduct a study initially to explore how racial bias might manifest itself in the personnel vetting process. Following the first phase of the study and initiation of the literature review, PAC PMO asked RAND authors to also explore the potential for bias and sources of inequity related to other areas, including gender, gender identity, sexual orientation, and neurodivergence (neurodiversity being the diversity of all cognitive functions). To that end in this study, we sought to

- review theories, practices, and studies within social sciences literature related to biases or sources of inequities regarding race or ethnicity, gender, gender identity, sexual orientation, and neurodivergence

---

[1] Note that this implementation strategy is updated on a quarterly basis; as of this writing, the latest version of the most recent update was released in March 2023.

- explore elements of the security clearance personnel vetting process in the context of such potential biases or inequities
- provide recommendations for policymaker consideration.

To identify potential aspects of the U.S. government personnel vetting process that may contribute to bias and sources of inequity, we first explored aspects of the structural element of the process—made up of rules, policies, procedures that shape the execution of the security clearance process—including (1) the Standard Form (SF) 86 (SF-86) questionnaire that candidates and staff are asked to fill out, which is ultimately submitted to an investigator to validate and pursue potential leads of information related to risk factors, and (2) the security clearance adjudicative guidelines (established in Security Executive Agent Directive 4 [SEAD-4], 2017), which identify risk factors an individual may present and provide the guidance for how the government should assess and adjudicate an individual. We then explored the human element of the process—made up of the views, experiences, actions, and judgments of people engaged in executing the security clearance process—including how perceptions and judgments of the investigators, adjudicators, and quality reviewers have the potential to affect the execution and outcome of the process. After analyzing these elements, we developed conclusions, observations, and recommendations for the government to consider related to addressing potential biases and sources of inequities in the personnel vetting process.

Approach and Methods

We conducted a two-pronged research approach for this study that consisted of (1) reviewing relevant literature related to bias and discrimination and (2) holding discussions with personnel vetting and DEIA experts about elements in the personnel vetting process that have the potential to contribute to bias and sources of inequity.

Literature Review

We conducted a descriptive literature review of research on racial differences in employment outcomes. That review was done in three phases. First, we conducted a keyword search of major research databases and identified 669 sources. This included journal articles, books, book chapters, and policy reports. Second, we conducted a title and abstract review of identified sources and excluded sources that were not relevant to our study. Third, we conducted a full-text review of relevant sources.

We also conducted narrative review of literature related to gender bias, LGBTQ+ bias, and neurodivergent bias in the workplace. For this review, we conducted keyword searches of research databases, reviewed results for relevance and conducted a limited full-text review of a subset of sources. Appendix B provides more details about the literature review methods and results.

Discussions

We held semistructured discussions with U.S. government personnel vetting experts and both U.S. government and private-sector DEIA experts about elements in the personnel vetting process that have the potential to contribute to racial or other bias; any ongoing diversity, equity, inclusion, and accessibility initiatives or training, in particular those related to the vetting process; any other relevant information that discussants were aware of on the topic; and any recommendations for areas for improvement. These subject-matter experts (SMEs) were drawn from a pool of potential participants who were either suggested by the project sponsor, were contacts within the team's network, or were identified via snowball sampling of recommended additional experts from our participants. Appendix C provides an anonymized summary list of discussants and the semistructured protocol guides used for the discussions. Appendix D provides further detail about the coding approach we used to analyze themes and findings derived from these discussions.

Structure of This Report

The remainder of this chapter provides background information related to definitions, prior research, and the key components of the personnel vetting process. Chapter 2 summarizes our descriptive literature review of theories and practices within the social sciences literature pertaining to bias related to race, as well as narrative review of literature related to gender, gender identity, sexual orientation, and neurodiversity. Chapter 3 summarizes observations and themes derived from our discussions with personnel vetting and DEIA experts. Chapter 4 offers our conclusion, observations, and recommendations for the government to consider related to addressing potential bias and sources of inequity in the personnel vetting process. We also include appendixes with an initial framing approach that could be used to start an evaluation of personnel vetting forms and adjudicative guidelines for potential areas of bias or inequity (Appendix A), a description of the methods used in our literature review (Appendix B), a anonymized summary list of discussants and the semistructured discussion protocol guides (Appendix C), and a summary of the coding scheme we used for the analysis of our semistructured discussions (Appendix D).

Definitions

We use several key terms to discuss the experiences of people of color, women, LGBTQ+ individuals, and neurodivergent individuals that are important to define at the outset:

- **Bias:** "partiality: an inclination or predisposition for or against something" (American Psychological Association, 2023)

- **Discrimination:** "the unfair or prejudicial treatment of people and groups based on characteristics such as race, gender, age or sexual orientation" (American Psychological Association, 2023)
- **Everyday racism and discrimination:** "differential treatment of individuals on the basis of their racial group that occurs in common, routine social situations" (American Psychological Association, 2023). Everyday discrimination expands on this concept and can include race, gender, and other categories of exclusion (Lewis et al., 2012; Williams et al., 1997).
- **Equity:** "the state, quality or ideal of being just, impartial and fair" (Annie E. Casey Foundation, 2015)
- **Neurodiversity:** "the variation in neurocognitive functioning. It is an umbrella term that encompasses neurocognitive differences such as autism, attention deficit/hyperactivity disorder (ADHD), dyslexia, Tourette's syndrome, anxiety, obsessive-compulsive disorder, depression, intellectual disability, and schizophrenia, as well as 'normal' neurocognitive functioning, or neurotypicality" (Employer Assistance and Resource Network on Disability Inclusion [EARN], undated)
- **Neurodivergent:** "those whose brain functions differ from those who are neurologically typical, or neurotypical"[2]
- **Structural racism and discrimination:** "refers to macro-level conditions (e.g. residential segregation and institutional policies) that limit opportunities, resources, power, and well-being of individuals and populations based on race/ethnicity and other statues, including but not limited to: gender, sexual orientation, gender identity, disability status, social class or socioeconomic status, religion, national origin, immigration status, limited English proficiency, physical characteristics or health outcomes" (National Institute on Minority Health and Health Disparities, 2022).

Previous Related Research

Past RAND research contains findings related to the potential for bias and inequity in the background investigation and personnel vetting processes. This research includes a 2022

---

[2] We leverage the same definition and logic as another recent RAND report, which noted the difficulty in distinguishing between neurodiversity, neurodivergence, and other related terms that continue to evolve through the academic literature:

> There is no authoritative definition for neurodivergence or neurodiversity, so we use the following: *Neurodiversity* refers to variation in neurocognitive functioning. It is an umbrella term that encompasses neurocognitive differences such as autism, attention deficit hyperactivity disorder (ADHD), dyslexia, Tourette's syndrome, anxiety, obsessive-compulsive disorder, depression, intellectual disability, and schizophrenia, as well as 'normal' neurocognitive functioning, or neurotypicality. Neurodivergent individuals are those whose brain functions differ from those who are neurologically typical, or neurotypical. (EARN, undated, as cited in Weinbaum et al., 2023)

study to determine the applicability and efficacy of using machine learning (ML) to detect signs of deception during investigative interviews, and a 2021 study focused on understanding emerging risks associated with new workforce generations (Posard et al., 2022; Posard et al., 2021). The ML study found that certain types of gender-based algorithm bias affects ML-detection accuracy, while the emerging risks report found that future iterations of the personnel vetting process will need to account for larger societal changes to ensure equity within the hiring process.

In 2022, RAND authors released an exploratory report specifically related to the potential for racial bias in the security clearance process. The study's purpose was to identify areas in the security clearance process where bias might present obstacles for Black Americans seeking a career within the federal government (Piquado et al., 2022). Those RAND authors found that

- nowhere in the security clearance process are data on race gathered, although data on race are collected during the hiring process; to assess the potential for racial disparities, data would have to be integrated from those two processes
- societal and human judgment factors might contribute to racial bias within the national security background process
- algorithm-based platforms that support process automation could surface biases, potentially as a result of programmer bias or historical racial differences
- individuals might not have a clear understanding of the information that is collected about them as part of the personnel vetting process, and how that information is used to make adjudicative decisions (Piquado et al., 2022).[3]

An Overview of Personnel Vetting Process

This section briefly describes the key components and phases of the U.S. government personnel vetting process. The personnel vetting process is a type of evaluation that seeks to establish whether an individual (a U.S. government candidate) should be trusted to protect classified, sensitive, or public trust related information. The types of data used to determine whether access should be granted include criminal history record information (CHRI), financial/credit history, and information about where the candidate has lived, worked, traveled, and associations with groups and individuals. Once a candidate has applied to and interviewed for a federal government position, the hiring organization submits a formal (sponsor) request to an investigative service provider (ISP) for investigative action. Which ISP conducts an investigation will vary dependent on what agency the candidate has applied to, but more

---

[3] For example, societal factors may include financial, drug-related, or criminal charges, while human judgement factors include affinity bias, confirmation bias, and statistical discrimination that "might contribute to racial bias in the security clearance process" (Piquado et al., 2022, p. 1).

than 95 percent of background investigations are conducted by the Defense Counterintelligence Security Agency (DCSA).[4] Once the background fieldwork investigation is completed, the investigative process may also include a quality review process that is intended to serve as an overall quality check (e.g., accuracy, completeness) for the investigation process; sometimes quality review can also occur in the process of a background investigation with *check rides*, in which a quality reviewer accompanies an investigator during the course of interviews (Farrell, 2017; Farrell, 2018).[5] Once the investigation process is complete, investigative *packages* are provided to an authorized adjudication agency (often the agency that submitted the investigative request) to make a determination of whether the individual can be trusted to protect people, property, information, and mission.

Adjudicators consult established adjudicative guidance to determine overall risks identified during the adjudication process. For the highest levels of vetting, which include evaluations of eligibility for security clearance, these guidelines include specific criteria used to determine conditions that may pose security risks, and factors that could mitigate security concerns to assess whether the *whole person*[6] should be granted clearance eligibility.[7] The adjudicative process may vary by adjudicative agency, but after adjudication, there is generally a quality review process to also serve as a check of this part of the process. Depending on the final adjudication determination (i.e., favorable versus unfavorable adjudication), the candidate may either begin entry on duty (EOD) at the hiring organization or may have the option to initiate a formal appeals process.

The federal personnel vetting process continues to modernize and evolve under the U.S. government's TW 2.0 initiative (see Figure 1.2). One key process change within the initiative includes moving from requiring a periodic reinvestigations (the same process described above happening approximately every five to ten years) to a continuous vetting program,

---

[4] EO 13869 (2019) and additional language in the 2019 National Defense Authorization Act transferred federal security clearance processing functions from OPM to DCSA. For additional information, see Defense Counterintelligence and Security Agency, undated-c; and Defense Counterintelligence and Security Agency, undated-a.

[5] The background investigation quality assurance process stage has been the subject of two recent GAO reports. For example, in 2017, GAO made several recommendations to the Director of National Intelligence and the Director of the National Background Investigations Bureau, one of which included "setting a milestone for establishing measures for investigation quality" (Farrell, 2018). See also Farrell, 2017.

[6] The *whole person* concept refers to a number of variables about a person's life being weighed to make an affirmative determination that the individual is an acceptable security risk (Office of the Director of National Intelligence, 2017). In practice, the concept means that no single issue will automatically result in security clearance denial or revocation without considering all other variables and aspects about the individual.

[7] In addition, the guidelines also state that "eligibility shall be determined by appropriately trained adjudicative personnel through the evaluation of all information bearing on an individual's loyalty and allegiance to the United States, including any information relevant to strength of character, honesty, discretion, sound judgment, reliability, ability to protect classified or sensitive information, and trustworthiness" (Office of the Director of National Intelligence, 2017).

FIGURE 1.2

Federal Personnel Vetting Process

SOURCE: Adapted from Defense Counterintelligence and Security Agency, undated-d.

which places all vetted government and contract staff to an automated alert–based system that queries multiple databases on a regular basis for derogatory information.[8] When a validated alert is received, focused investigations are then conducted into the specific issue, and an individual's eligibility is readjudicated in the context of the new information and with the application of the whole person adjudicative concept.

Background Investigation and Investigation Forms and Questionnaires

Background investigations are required to gather the necessary information to make a trust determination at the level required based on the assigned position designation. National security positions require access to classified information; background investigations for national security positions require the candidate to fill out the SF-86 questionnaire (OPM, 2016).[9] Background investigations for nonsensitive positions require the candidate to fill out the SF-85, while positions for public trust require the candidate to fill out the SF-85P, and selected positions also require the SF-85P-S to be submitted (OPM, 2017a; OPM, 2017b; OPM, 2017c). Although nonsensitive and public trust positions represent a substantial portion of the U.S. government–vetted workforce, we decided to focus this study's analysis primarily on the national security population and the associated SF-86 form. This decision is partly because the SF-86, 85, 85-P, and 85P-S forms request a great deal of the same categories of information across forms, but the SF-86 is the most comprehensive and expansive of the SF questionnaires related to personnel vetting. Additionally, the SF-86 questionnaire is intended to collect information to inform adjudication based on the associated SEAD-4 adjudicative guidelines.[10]

---

[8] For example, the new system would query U.S. government databases containing information related to terrorism, foreign travel, financial activity, criminal activity, credit history, and other public records that assess continuing eligibility for access to national security (or other sensitive) information. For more information, see DCSA, undated-b.

[9] The SF-86 may be viewed at OPM, 2016.

[10] In November 2022, the OPM submitted a "Notice of Submission for a New Information Collection Common Form: Personnel Vetting Questionnaire." This *common form* (or Personnel Vetting Questionnaire [PVQ]), if adopted, would make changes to certain aspects of the information collected through the various SF-85 and SF-86 forms. However, our study focused on the existing and current SF forms in active

The SF-86 contains 29 sections of questions, which we categorized into five overall themes: establishing candidate identification, establishing candidate credentials, establishing candidate relationships and networks, establishing external influence, and establishing additional factors related to risk behaviors. The sections of the SF-86, along with our associated categorizations, are summarized in Table 1.1.

Establishing Candidate Identification

SF-86 questions in this category focus on verifying the candidate's name, date of birth, place of birth, Social Security number, personal identifying information (height, weight, hair color, eye color), and binary sex categorizations male or female, along with U.S. citizenship and previous living locations.[11] The primary purpose of these initial sections are to ensure that the applicant has legal citizenship status within the United States and to help investigators perform database records checks using the provided identifiable information (Ligor et al., 2022).

Establishing Candidate Credentials

Baseline questions in this category seek to understand what schools candidates have attended, employment activities, Selective Service registration, and general military history (if applicable). These series of questions serve a variety of functions within the vetting process; school or university attendance records provide investigators with additional points of contact that may be used for follow-up discussions about the applicant's academic honesty, attendance, and other demeanor during their time at the institution. Employment activity data provide investigators with an opportunity to speak to coworkers and managers, and also supply additional information related to firing, quitting, misconduct, and other employment related issues that investigators may vet against form-provided responses.[12]

Establishing Candidate Relationships and Networks

Sections 16, 17, and 18 ask applicants to list and provide contact information for friends, spouses, partners, cohabitants, marriage or relationship status, and close relatives (e.g., sib-

---

use at the time of this study. We will address some of the relevant changes proposed in the PVQ (common form) later in this report.

[11] 32 CFR, Part 2001 (*Classified National Security Information*) provides U.S. citizenship requirements for access to national security information. 32 CFR is derived from EO 13526. DCSA (undated-e) notes that,

> If a non-U.S. citizen requires access to U.S. classified information and meets the requirements of the 32 Code of Federal Regulations (CFR) 117.10(k), a Limited Access Authorization (LAA) no higher than the Secret level may be issued. An LAA enables a non U.S. citizen to have limited access to classified information, but the LAA is not a national security eligibility. Access to classified will be limited to a specific program or project and will be cancelled upon the completion of the program or project for which it was approved.

[12] Employment-related questions may include, "Have you received a written warning, been officially reprimanded, suspended, or disciplined for misconduct in the workplace, such as a violation of security policy?" followed by a listing of justifications: "Provide the reason(s) for being warned, reprimanded, suspended or disciplined" (see more SF-86 questions at OPM, 2016).

TABLE 1.1
Standard Form 86 Question Categories

Question Theme	Question Category
Establish Candidate Identification	Sections 1–5: Full Name, Date of Birth, Place of Birth, Social Security Number, Other Names Used
	Section 6: Identifying Information (Height, Weight, Hair Color, Eye Color, Sex [Male/Female])
	Section 7: Contact Information (phone, email)
	Section 8: U.S. Passport Information
	Section 9: Citizenship
	Section 10: Dual/Multiple Citizenship & Foreign Passport Information
	Section 11: Where You Have Lived
Establish Candidate Credentials	Section 12: Where You Went to school
	Section 13A/B: Employment Activities
	Section 14: Selective Service Record
	Section 15: Military History
Establish Candidate Relationships/Networks	Section 16: People Who Know You Well
	Section 17: Marital/Relationship Status
	Section 18: Relatives
Establish External Influence	Section 19: Foreign Contacts
	Section 20A/B/C: Foreign Activities/Foreign Business, Professional Activities, and Foreign Government Contacts/Foreign Travel
Establish Additional Factors Related to Risk Behaviors	Section 21A/B/C/D/E: Psychological and Emotional Health
	Section 22: Police Record
	Section 23: Illegal Use of Drugs and Drug Activity
	Section 24: Use of Alcohol
	Section 25: Investigations and Clearance Record
	Section 26: Financial Record
	Section 27: Use of IT Systems
	Section 28: Involvement in Non-Criminal Court Actions
	Section 29: Association Record

SOURCE: Features information from OPM, 2016.

lings, parents, children). These sections serve to complement information derived from speaking with teachers, coworkers, or neighbors provided in earlier sections. The form directs applicants to list individuals who are "collectively aware" of "activities outside of your workplace, school, or neighborhood, and whose combined association with you covers at least the last seven (7) years" (OPM, 2016, p. 35). Although investigators generally speak with individuals listed on the form, the investigator may also generate additional points of contact from discussions to ensure that adjudicators have an accurate portrayal of the candidate in subsequent vetting stages.

Establishing External Influence

Sections 19 and 20 ask candidates to supply information about foreign contacts, foreign activities (e.g., foreign business, professional activities), association with foreign government contacts, and all instances of foreign travel, regardless of personal or business purposes. The primary purpose of these sections are to better understand whether the applicant may be prone to external (foreign) influence that could present risk. For example, listed contacts in this section might be further explored to see whether (1) the applicant may have relationships with foreign intelligence entities; (2) the applicant may be prone to blackmail activity; or (3) whether the applicant has close and continuing contact with other known U.S. adversaries.[13]

Establishing Additional Factors Related to Risk Behaviors

Sections 21 through 26 ask applicants to list previous or ongoing issues related to psychological and emotional health, criminal history, use of drugs and drug activity, use of alcohol, previous investigation, and clearance decisions (if applicable), financial stability, use of information technology (IT) systems, involvement in noncriminal court actions, and other associations that may present risk to a position. Questions in this section focus on the frequency and recency of derogatory activity—and whether the candidate voluntarily sought professional assistance to manage criminal, mental health, or substance abuse related issues. Although information reported in this section may not automatically disqualify eligibility to access national security information, the circumstances (e.g., voluntary versus court mandated) are important in the adjudication phase.

Adjudication and Adjudicative Guidelines

After the investigation phase, the candidate's package moves on to adjudication, so this section briefly describes the role of adjudicators and adjudicative guidance in the personnel vetting process. Table 1.2 provides an overview of the 13 existing adjudicative guidelines, derived from SEAD-4. The adjudication process occurs once the information contained in

---

[13] Close and continuing contact is assessed through the following frequencies: daily, weekly, monthly, quarterly, or annually.

TABLE 1.2
SEAD-4 Adjudicative Guidelines Overview

Adjudicative Guideline	Primary Concerns
Guideline A–Allegiance to the United States	An individual must be of unquestioned allegiance to the United States. The willingness to safeguard classified information is in doubt if there is any reason to suspect an individual's allegiance to the United States.
Guideline B–Foreign Influence	A security risk may exist when an individual's immediate family, including cohabitants and other persons to whom he or she may be bound by affection, influence, or obligation, are not citizens of the United States or may be subject to duress.
Guideline C–Foreign Preference	When an individual acts in such a way as to indicate a preference for a foreign country over the United States, then he or she may be prone to provide information or make decisions that are harmful to the interests of the United States.
Guideline D–Sexual Behavior	Sexual behavior is a security concern if it involves a criminal offense; indicates a personality or emotional disorder; may subject the individual to coercion, exploitation, or duress; or reflects lack of judgment or discretion. Sexual orientation or preference may not be used as a basis for or a disqualifying factor in determining a person's eligibility for a security clearance
Guideline E–Personal Conduct	Conduct involving questionable judgment, untrustworthiness, unreliability, lack of candor, dishonesty, or unwillingness to comply with rules and regulations could indicate that the person may not properly safeguard classified information.
Guideline F–Financial Considerations	An individual who is financially overextended is at risk of having to engage in illegal acts to generate funds. Unexplained affluence is often linked to proceeds from financially profitable criminal acts.
Guideline G–Alcohol Consumption	Excessive alcohol consumption often leads to the exercise of questionable judgment, unreliability, and failure to control impulses and increases the risk of unauthorized disclosure of classified information due to carelessness.
Guideline H–Drug Involvement	Improper or illegal involvement with drugs raises questions regarding an individual's willingness or ability to protect classified information. Drug abuse or dependence may impair social or occupational functioning, increasing the risk of an unauthorized disclosure of classified information.
Guideline I–Emotional, Mental, and Personality Disorders	Emotional, mental, and personality disorders can cause a significant deficit in an individual's psychological, social and occupation functioning. These disorders are of security concern because they may indicate a defect in judgment, reliability, or stability.
Guideline J–Criminal Conduct	A history or pattern of criminal activity creates doubt about a person's judgment, reliability, and trustworthiness.
Guideline K–Security Violations	Noncompliance with security regulations raises doubt about an individual's trustworthiness, willingness, and ability to safeguard classified information.
Guideline L–Outside Activities	Involvement in certain types of outside employment or activities is of security concern if it poses a conflict with an individual's security responsibilities and could create an increased risk of unauthorized disclosure of classified information.

Table 1.2—Continued

Adjudicative Guideline	Primary Concerns
Guideline M–Misuse of Information Technology Systems	Noncompliance with rules, procedures, guidelines, or regulations pertaining to information technology systems may raise security concerns about an individual's trustworthiness, willingness, and ability to properly protect classified systems, networks, and information.

SOURCE: Features information from Office of the Director of Intelligence, 2017; CFR 32, Part 147.

the security questionnaire has been investigated and validated by an investigator.[14] Per the SEAD-4 guidelines and CFR 32 Part 147, the adjudications process is "an examination of a sufficient period of a person's life to make an affirmative determination that the person is eligible for a security clearance" (Office of the Director of National Intelligence, 2017; CFR 32, Part 147).[15] Cases that receive a favorable adjudication about eligibility for access to U.S. government national security (or sensitive) information are then provided back to hiring organizations with the appropriate eligibility determination.[16] Cases that receive an unfavorable determination may be formally appealed by the candidate through the appropriate administrative process, based on the hiring agency and the responsible appeals authority.

Conditions That Could Raise Security Concerns

There are several different risk factors listed across each of the 13 adjudicative guidelines within SEAD-4 that may cause security concerns related to access. These concerns include a willingness to safeguard classified or sensitive information, potential for manipulation (or coercion) by foreign entities, or previous actions that may raise questions about an individual's ability to "comply with laws, rules, and regulations" (Office of the Director of Intelligence, 2017). The guidelines also provide a listing of other contextual information that is intended to help adjudicators determine the extent or seriousness (e.g., recency) of derogatory information. The guidelines detail that certain types of behavior or prior acts may be indicative of a general lack of judgement or discretion, lack of candor, a failure to control impulses, and overall reliability, which assist adjudicators in rendering a final determination.

---

[14] The investigator may also conduct a preliminary security interview prior to the start of the investigation to clarify potential issues listed on security forms—or to gain additional information as needed.

[15] Furthermore, CFR 32, Part 147, notes that

> Eligibility for access to classified information is predicated upon the individual meeting these personnel security guidelines. The adjudicative process is the careful weighing of a number of variables known as the whole person concept. Available, reliable information about the person, past and present, favorable and unfavorable, should be considered in reaching a determination.

[16] A full listing of eligibility consideration, including temporary eligibility, please see CFR 32.

Conditions That Could Mitigate Security Concerns

In SEAD-4, each of the conditions that could raise security concerns during the adjudicative process also have a separate listing of mitigating factors to assist adjudicators in evaluating candidates from a holistic (i.e., whole person) perspective (Kyzer, 2019). Key mitigating factors include

1. the "nature, extent, and seriousness" of the conduct in question
2. the "circumstances surrounding the conduct, to include knowledgeable participation"
3. the "frequency and recency of the conduct"
4. the "individuals age and maturity at the time of the conduct"
5. the "extent to which participation is voluntary"
6. the "presence or absence of rehabilitation and other permanent behavioral changes"
7. motivations underlying the conduct in question"
8. the "potential for pressure, coercion, exploitation, or duress" that could pose risks to specific national security positions
9. and the "likelihood of continuation or recurrence" (Office of the Director of Intelligence, 2017).

Additional mitigating circumstances may include how the derogatory information was reported (e.g., self-reported versus a police investigation), whether the candidate was forthcoming during investigator questioning, and whether the candidate has established a documented record of recovery and/or no evidence of criminal recurrence.[17]

Summary

In this introductory chapter, we provided an overview of our research methods and approach; summarized recent U.S. government actions and polices prioritizing DEIA initiatives, including those related to the federal national security workforce; and discussed other relevant research regarding the potential for bias within the security clearance and background investigation process. We also described key components of the personnel vetting process and summarized the U.S. government–identified conditions that may raise security concerns as individuals are investigated for security clearance eligibility, along with the set of mitigating factors that authorized adjudicative agencies use to determine overall risk to that an individual might present. With this understanding of the personnel vetting process that applicants are required to go through, we now turn to our literature review, which explores the employment factors and workplace discrimination that can limit professional opportunities for people of color, women, LGBTQ+ individuals, and neurodivergent individuals.

---

[17] SEAD-4 defines these last factors as "demonstrated positive changes in behavior" (Office of the Director of Intelligence, 2017).

CHAPTER 2

Literature Review

This chapter discusses previous research on employment and workplace discrimination. Although our main literature review focused primarily on racial discrimination in the workplace, we also provide brief discussions from an exploratory review of research on gender, gender identity, sexual orientation (LGBTQ+), and neurodivergent discrimination in employment. We focus on the ways that structural factors and individual-level discrimination can limit professional opportunities and workplace treatment for people of color, women, LGBTQ+ individuals, and neurodivergent individuals. The research here is important for informing the analysis of potential factors of bias and sources of inequity and barriers in the security clearance process, which is a required part of the employment process for national security professionals.

Approach and Methods

We conducted a descriptive review of literature review of research on racial differences in employment outcomes.[1] Keywords for this search included "employment," "discrimination," "job applicant screening," and "race." Database searches included Scopus, Business Source Complete, APA PsychInfo, Web of Science, and Sociological Abstracts. Search results were limited to research published between 2002 and 2022.[2] In total, the search yielded 669 sources. Once the search was complete, we conducted a three-phase review of the sources using DistillerSR literature review software.[3] In the first phase, we reviewed the title and abstract of each source and excluded sources that were not focused on racial differences in labor market outcomes and any duplicate sources. In the second phase, we conducted a second title and abstract review to exclude any sources that were not focused on the hiring process because of

---

[1] Paré and Kitsiou (2017) define a *descriptive literature review* as a review that is structured to "determine the extent to which a body of knowledge in a particular research topic reveals any interpretable pattern or trend with respect to pre-existing propositions, theories, methodologies or findings." Descriptive reviews include a systematic search strategy and screening procedure (see Paré and Kitsiou, 2017).

[2] Our literature review was conducted in May 2022, and we included sources published between 2002 and 2022 to capture research published in the 20 years prior to our study.

[3] DistillerSR (undated) is a software program designed to conduct literature reviews. The software allows for the systematic review of a large number of sources by a multiperson research team.

this study's focus on hiring. In the third phase, we conducted a full-text review of each source, summarizing methods and main findings.

Although the initial and primary focus of this study is on the potential for racial bias, we also conducted an narrative review of literature on gender bias, LGBTQ+ bias, and neurodivergent bias in employment, based in part on sponsor interest in the study team further exploring these topics.[4] For these topics, informal keyword searches were conducted to identify relevant literature, and limited full-text reviews of identified sources were reviewed. Appendix B provides more details about the literature review methods and results.

Race and Ethnicity Employment Literature

Research consistently shows that people of color have significantly different labor market experiences and outcomes than White applicants in the United States (Bertrand and Mullainathan, 2004; Pager and Shepherd, 2008; Quillian, Lee, and Oliver, 2020; Wilson and Darity, 2022). The persistent racial wage gap—particularly between White workers and African American workers and White workers and Latino workers—is one indicator of racial inequality in the labor market (Kochhar and Cilluffo, 2018; U.S. Department of Labor, undated; Wilson and Darity, 2022). For example, the U.S. Department of Labor (undated) notes that African American workers earn 76 cents for every $1 that White workers earn, and Latino workers earn 73 cents for every $1 that White workers earn. Previous research has shown that racial wage gaps persist regardless of level of education or skills (U.S. Department of Labor, undated). Racial wage gaps also persist in all areas of the labor market (Wilson and Darity, 2022).

A substantial body of research has focused on understanding the factors that contribute to these racial differences in labor market outcomes (e.g., Bertrand and Mullainathan, 2004; Pager and Shepherd, 2008; Quillian, Lee, and Oliver, 2020; Wilson and Darity, 2022). We reviewed research on discrimination in the labor market, focusing on discrimination in hiring because that process occurs pre-employment, just as security clearance vetting occurs prior to individuals starting in their national security positions. This review identifies *potential* sources of bias that could arise during the security clearance process. In this section, we explore research racial differences in hiring and the sources of these differences, which include structural factors, statistical discrimination, and individual-level racism.

---

[4] Paré and Kitsiou (2017) explain that "a narrative review attempts to summarize or synthesize what has been written on a particular topic." However, sources are not reviewed using a systematic set of criteria unlike a larger, systematic review.

Racial Differences in Hiring

This section provides an overview of research that explores racial differences at different phases of the hiring process. We focus on racial differences in who gets called back for jobs after applying for openings and who gets job offers after interviewing for positions.

Getting Called Back

There is a large body of research that demonstrates persistent racial differences in how applications are evaluated, which affects who gets called back for jobs. For example, Pager, Bonisowski, and Western (2009) conducted a field experiment to examine discrimination in the low-wage labor market and found evidence of racial discrimination and discrimination against job applicants with criminal records. White, Black, and Latino test applicants were assigned to apply for 340 real job listings in New York City. Testers were given fictitious resumes that were matched according to various characteristics, including educational attainment and previous work experience. Testers also completed a job training program to ensure unified behavior across applicants. The authors found that White applicants received callbacks 31 percent of the time, compared with 25.2 percent of the time for Latino applicants and 15.2 percent for Black applicants (Pager, Bonisowski, and Western, 2009).

Bertrand and Mullainathan (2004) compared callbacks for applicants with names more prevalent among African American job-seekers and names more prevalent among White candidates.[5] They drew from a pool of real résumés to create a sample of fictitious résumés to apply for jobs in sales, administrative support, clerical services, and customer services in Boston and Chicago. Each résumé was assigned an "African American" or "White" name. They also divided the sample of résumés into high quality and low quality. High-quality résumés had more experience and skills than lower-quality résumés. In total, they sent out approximately 5,000 résumés to 1,300 job openings. They found that applicants with African American names were 50 percent less likely than applicants with White names to receive a callback after applying for a job. In addition, although White applicants were 27 percent more likely to receive a callback when they had a higher-quality résumé, African American applicants were only 8 percent more likely to receive a callback with a higher-quality résumé. This finding suggests that when applicants are perceived as African American job-seekers, they may not receive the same benefit from having more credentials than White applicants do.

Quillian, Lee, and Oliver (2020) conducted a meta-analysis of 12 field experiment studies on racial discrimination in the labor market. All of the studies they reviewed explored racial

---

[5] To categorize the names of African American and White applicants, the authors constructed a database of names of babies born in Massachusetts between 1974 and 1979. They matched each name to the race of the baby born and developed a list of names that were most prevalent among African American applicants and a list of names that were most prevalent among White applicants. To validate the list, they also surveyed 30 respondents in Chicago about the race associated with each name. The list of names categorized for African American applicants included Aisha, Tanisha, Darnell, and Jamal. The list of names categorized for White applicants included Emily, Kristin, Todd, and Brad.

differences in callbacks for job applicants. They found that, across the 12 studies, White applicants received callbacks 53 percent more often than White applicants.

Getting a Job Offer

When applicants are called back, discrimination has also been found to persist through the interview process. For example, in their audit of hiring in the low-wage labor market, Pager, Bonikowski, and Western (2009) also found significant racial differences in job interviews. They found that when applicants did reach an interview phase, Black and Latino applicants were more likely to be steered toward lower-paying positions with fewer opportunities for advancement. In contrast, they found that, in several cases, White applicants were more likely to be steered toward higher-level positions, such as managerial and supervisory roles. These actions occurred despite applicants from different racial backgrounds having similar educational and employment backgrounds. Bendick, Rodriguez, and Jayaraman (2010) compared the experiences of White and racial minority job applicants seeking waiter/waitress positions at high-end restaurants in New York City. They used 37 testers to apply for open jobs. Testers were paired into teams (one with White applicants and one with racial minority applicants),[6] and each pair applied for open waiter/waitress positions. Pairs were given similar resumes with the same amount of education and work experience. The researchers completed a total of 138 tests and found that around 81 percent of White applicants received a job interview, compared with around 61 percent of minority applicants. In addition, they found that about 31 percent of White applicants received a job offer compared with approximately 19 percent of minorities. Findings demonstrate significant differences in the experiences of White and minority applicants. The authors also note that these experiences have important consequences for occupational sorting and earnings because higher-end restaurants pay more, and their findings show that White applicants were significantly more likely to be hired for these positions.

Assessing Potential Causes for Racial Differences in Hiring

This section provides an overview of research that examines factors that contribute to racial differences in hiring. We discuss such structural factors as individual background characteristics, the prevalence of statistical discrimination and the persistence of everyday racism.

Structural Factors and Statistical Discrimination

Research has shown that some job selection criteria may contribute to racial differences in job market outcomes. One aspect of the job selection process that has received considerable attention from previous research is criminal background checks. 1 Half and Ten and The Sentencing Project (2022) estimates that 100 million Americans have criminal records. This

---

[6] Bendick, Rodriguez, and Jayaraman (2010) define *minority* as a Black, Hispanic, Asian, or Middle Eastern person.

means that a substantial portion of the population may have a criminal record when applying for a job. In addition, African American and Latino men are particularly likely to have a criminal record. For example, Brame et al. (2014) used the data from National Longitudinal Survey of Youth to examine the arrest record prevalence among African American, White, and Latino men ages 18–23. They found that by age 23, 48.9 percent of African American men and 43.8 percent of Latino men had been arrested, compared with 38 percent of White males. Using data from the Bureau of Justice Statistics, the 1 Half and Ten and The Sentencing Project (2022) found that African American men are six times more likely to be incarcerated than White men and that Latino men are 2.5 times more likely to be incarcerated than White men. Thus, non-White men may be disproportionately affected by criminal background checks in job searches and background investigations (Alexander, 2010; Emory, 2021; Pager, Bonikowski, and Western, 2009; Vuolo, Lageson, and Uggen, 2017; Wakefield and Uggen, 2010).

Pager (2003) explored the impact of having been incarcerated on Black and White male job applicants. The author conducted an audit study, using four male testers to apply for entry-level jobs in the Milwaukee, Wisconsin, metropolitan area. Testers were paired by race, and one tester in each pair was assigned a criminal record, while the other had no criminal record. *Criminal record* was defined as a prior drug conviction and having served 18 months in prison. Pairs were matched on other characteristics, such as work history and educational attainment. In total, they applied to actual job openings with 350 employers in the area. For the White pair, the applicant without a criminal record received a callback 34 percent of the time, compared with 17 percent of the time for the applicant with a criminal record. For the Black pair, the applicant without a criminal record received a callback 17 percent of the time, compared with 5 percent of the time for the applicant with a criminal record. The results show the persistence of racial discrimination in the labor market, the impact of having a criminal history on labor market outcomes, and the intersection of race and criminal history.

Similarly, the audit study by Pager, Bonikowski, and Western (2009) found that job applicants with a felony conviction were significantly less likely to receive callbacks than those without felony convictions. When testers' fictitious résumés were given a criminal record, White applicants with a felony conviction received callbacks around 17 percent of the time, compared with around 15 percent for Latino applicants and 13 percent for Black applicants.

Research has also explored the impact that credit checks in the job application process may have on racial differences in employment outcomes (Ballance, Clifford, and Shoag, 2020; Volpone et al., 2015). Authors conducted Monte Carlo simulations to explore the impact of using credit scores on the hiring outcomes of African American and White job applicants (Volpone et al., 2015). Across models, they found that fewer African American applicants than White applicants were hired when Fair Isaac Corporation (FICO) credit scores were used. They experimented with different cutoff points for credit scores in applicant screening and found that lowering the threshold to 550—which is the lower end of the credit score distribution in the United States—still resulted in fewer African American applicants being hired.[7]

Research has also shown that employers may use broader structural trends to make hiring decisions, which is defined as *statistical discrimination*. Quillian, Lee, and Oliver (2020) argue that statistical discrimination plays a significant role in employer's decisions. This means that they make decisions in screening based on the use of "average characteristics of employees from different racial groups to draw conclusions about individual prospective employees based on their race" (Quillian, Lee, and Oliver, 2020, p. 735). Thus, an employer may decide about hiring an individual from a particular racial group based on their understanding of broader statistics about that group as opposed to fully evaluating the individual's job application.

The impact of statistical discrimination has been evident in a growing body of research examining the impact of "ban the box" policies. Some of this research has shown that removing questions about criminal history form job applications does not improve job prospects for people with criminal records, particularly African American and Latino applicants. Research has argued that this is in part because of persistent statistical discrimination, meaning that employers make continue to make decisions about job applicants based on their own assessment of their likelihood of having a criminal record (Emory, 2021; Sabia et al., 2021).

For example, Emory (2021) found that the implementation of ban the box policies can have a negative impact on men with criminal records. Using data from the Fragile Families study and longitudinal state-level data on the implementation of criminal record employment policies, they found that when policies are implemented that restrict the questions about criminal background on job applications, men with criminal backgrounds are less likely to be employed. In addition, African American men without a criminal record are also less likely to be employed. Emory (2021) argue this is because employers engage in statistical discrimination when they are unable to ask job applicants about their criminal histories, which actually increases the likelihood of exclusion from job opportunities for men with criminal histories and African American men (who employers believe are more likely to have criminal records, even when they do not).

Vuolo et al. (2017) examined how job application questions about criminal record can affect the employment prospects of applicants by conducting a two-part audit. First, they sent out 605 applications to randomly selected job openings in the Twin Cities, Minnesota, metropolitan area. Two same-race applications were sent out to each job opening. In each case, one applicant had no criminal history and one had a low-level misdemeanor offense. Second, they used eight male testers to apply for job openings over the course of several months. One

---

[7]   An estimated 90 percent of people in the United States have a credit score that is higher than 550 (Volpone et al., 2015). However, it is also important to note that credit scores vary significantly by race. For example, Garon (2022) found that adults ages 25 to 29 living in predominantly African American neighborhoods have a median credit score of 582, compared with a median score of 644 for those living in predominantly Latino neighborhoods and a median score of 687 for those living in predominantly White neighborhoods.

pair was assigned a misdemeanor offense as part of its background, while the other pair was assigned no offence. The testers were grouped in pairs and matched by race. In total, pairs completed approximately 300 applications at 150 different workplaces. The researchers found that, regardless of criminal history, African American applicants were least likely to be called back. However, they also found that the racial gap in callbacks was smaller when employers asked detailed questions on the application about criminal history, suggesting that statistical discrimination may affect applicants.

Although much of the research on criminal records and employment focuses on lower-skilled positions, recent research demonstrates that having a criminal record can also negatively affect the job prospects of individuals with a college degree, particularly African American applicants. Cerda-Jara, Elster, and Harding (2020) examined how having a criminal record affects the job prospects of college-educated, formerly incarcerated men. They created 1,798 fictitious résumés and cover letters and used them to submit applications for industry jobs. They found that 8 percent of applicants with a bachelor's degree and no criminal record received a callback after applying for a job. In contrast, 4 percent of applicants with a bachelor's degree and a criminal record received a callback after applying for a job. In addition, 4 percent of applicants who had not completed a bachelor's degree and had a criminal record received callback after applying for a job. Thus, applicants with a criminal record and a bachelor's degree did not fare better than applicants with a criminal record who had not completed a bachelor's degree.

Ballance, Clifford, and Shoag (2020) found a similar trend when employers are prevented from using credit scores in the job screening process. The authors used national data from Equifax, the Federal Reserve Bank of New York Consumer Credit Panel, and Longitudinal Employer-Household Dynamics Origin-Destination Employment Statistics. The researchers found that in areas where employers are prevented from using credit checks, a greater share of the employed population resides in what they define as *lower-risk geographic areas*. These are census tracts with the lowest percentages of people with major derogatory accounts and past-due debts. Thus, the researchers argue that employers may engage in statistical discrimination when they are unable to use credit checks as part of the screening process, negatively affecting people who live in less financially stable areas.

Everyday Racism

Research has also shown that people of color face frequent experiences with everyday racism that can affect their employment outcomes. These are often individual-level incidents that include various forms of racial bias that result in exclusion from opportunities at all levels (Bendick, Rodriguez, and Jayaraman, 2010; Feagin, 1995; Lamont et al., 2016; Caminiti, 2022; Mong and Roscigno, 2010; Wingfield and Chavez, 2020). Previous research has shown that in the job application process, racial minorities' experiences can range widely, from being underestimated to facing shifting standards in the interview process.

For example, Mong and Roscigno's 2010 study explores discrimination suits filed by African American men with the Ohio Civil Rights Commission (OCRC) between 1998 and 2003. Of the cases filed, around 4 percent were focused on hiring. Complainants reported several issues that centered on subjective, negative evaluations of applicants of color. For example, one applicant applied for a position as a grounds keeper for a public school system that required a written and oral exam. Although the applicant was told he had the highest score of any applicant on the written exam, he received low scores on the oral exam (which involved more-subjective evaluations). As a result, the applicant did not receive a job offer. In another case, a welder applied for a job at a business that stated that welding experience was required for the position. However, when he arrived for the position he was told that the job ad was incorrect and he actually needed welding *and* electrician experience. Because he did not have experience as an electrician, he was turned away and told that the company would correct the job ad for future applicants. Both cases ended with a favorable finding for the complainant, meaning that the OCRC found validity in its claims.

Wingfield and Chavez (2020) drew from 60 in-depth interviews with doctors, nurses, and medical technicians to explore the prevalence of racial discrimination in medicine. They found that nurses, in particular, reported experiences with discrimination during hiring. For example, one respondent felt that some interviewers were less likely to positively evaluate job candidates who attended historically Black colleges and universities (HBCUs) than candidates who attended predominantly White universities (PWIs). As a result, African American applicants, who were more likely to have degrees from HBCUs, were less likely to be hired for nursing positions.

Bendick, Rodriguez, and Jayaraman's 2010 study of hiring in upscale New York City restaurants, which found that White job applicants fared better than racial minorities, also explored applicants' perceptions of their interactions with interviewers. They found that, in general, racial minority applicants reported less friendly interactions and more scrutiny from interviewers. For example, about 86 percent of White applicants reported that the interviewer shook their hand, compared with around 74 percent of racial minority applicants who reported on the same interaction. In addition, about 76 percent of racial minority applicants reported being asked probing questions about their knowledge of food, wine, and table service, compared with almost 67 percent of White applicants being asked the same questions. The authors found that, cumulatively, these issues created significant differences in how White and racial minority applicants were treated by interviewers.

In summary, research has demonstrated that people of color face significant discrimination in the hiring process. This finding includes being less likely to be called back for job openings, being less likely to be hired for jobs if they receive an interview, and being hired for lower-level positions than White applicants. There are several factors that contribute to persistent discrimination. Structural inequalities can have a negative impact on minority job applicants, such as disproportionate criminal justice system contacts and use of credit reports in background checks. Research has also shown that employers engage in statistical discrimination, meaning that they discriminate against racial minorities based on broader trends, such as the percentage of people of color who have a criminal record. In addition, people of color report persistent experiences with individual-level racism during the hiring process that can affect their job opportunities. It is also important to emphasize that previous research shows that discrimination can occur across the labor market in a variety of positions. This is important because job listings for cleared positions can range from janitor to engineer (for examples, see listings for cleared jobs on clearancejobs.net).

Gender, Gender Identity, and Sexual Orientation Employment Literature

Research has also shown that gender discrimination can significantly affect employment outcomes. In the United States, on average, women earn 83 percent of what men earn (Institute for Women's Policy Research, 2022). Research has continuously shown that the wage gap persists, even when controlling background factors such as skills and level of education. As with racial discrimination, gender discrimination can occur at any phase in the employment process, affecting whether individuals are hired and the types of jobs they are hired to perform.

There are several sources of potential gender bias. Heilman (2012) argues that stereotypes can contribute to differential employment trajectories for men and women. Specifically, beliefs about women's attributes and their fit for certain positions can shape who gets hired (and later promoted) for certain positions. Jobs that are stereotyped as "male jobs" can be harder for women to obtain. Hess (2013) studied nonverbal sex discrimination in simulated job interviews. The author conducted mock job interviews using 22 interviewers and 107 interviewees. Interviews were videotaped and coded for nonverbal communications, such as whether or not the interviewer smiled frequently, made eye contact with the interviewee, and had relaxed and open arms during the interview (all determined categorized as more positive behaviors). Applicants interviewed for hypothetical jobs including elementary teacher, interior designer, and engineer. Hess found that, overall, more-experienced interviewers displayed fewer positive behaviors toward women interviewing for jobs that were viewed as more stereotypically male jobs, such as an engineer.

Heilman (2001) argues that gender stereotypes can contribute to bias in performance evaluations, limiting opportunities for occupation mobility for women. Specifically, Heilman notes that that descriptive and prescriptive stereotypes can affect performance evaluations because they can shape what employers view as the most-desirable traits for employees, particularly in upper-level positions. For example, attributes more typically used to describe men may be listed as most desirable for a management-level position. However, because evaluators are less likely to use these attributes to describe women, they face more challenges in seeking upper-level positions.[8]

---

[8] Heilman defines *descriptive stereotypes* as those that assign different sets of attributes to men and women. For example, Heilman explains that men may be described with such words as "forceful" and "indepen-

Biases about caregiving responsibilities can play an important role in an employer's perceptions of women. Caregivers are less likely to be hired, rated less competent and rated as less committed than non-caregivers. Additionally, female caregivers are perceived less favorably than male caregivers (Henle et al., 2020; Heilman and Okimoto, 2008). For example, Heilman and Okimoto (2008) conducted two experimental studies examining the potential impact of bias against parents. Study 1 asked 65 male and female undergraduate college students (average age 19 years) to evaluate four job applicants for promotion within a company—one male parent, one female parent, one male nonparent and one female nonparent (the applicant materials and job descriptions were constructed for the study by the researchers). Participants were asked to rate applicants on anticipated job commitment and anticipated competence. The authors found that while study participants rated both male and female applicants who were parents lower than nonparents on job commitment measures, only female parents received ratings on competence measures (Heilman and Okimoto, 2008). For Study 2, they replicated Study 1 with 100 master of business of administration students (average age 28.2 years) and found similar results, demonstrating that views persisted among older evaluators.

England (2010) also argues that although gender inequality in the United States has decreased since the middle of the 20th century, this progress has been uneven. Levels of educational attainment and employment for women have increased significantly since the 1960s, but England emphasizes that much of the movement has been focused on increasing the representation of women in traditionally male-dominated spaces. Little progress has been made in changing the construction of spaces that have been historically dominated by women. These areas include caregiving spaces and jobs that are disproportionately performed by women. For example, although more women may work in science, technology, engineering, and math (STEM) fields than during the middle of the 20th century, women also remain more likely than men to take on caregiving responsibilities for children than men. As a result, gender stereotypes persist, and they can continue to limit opportunities for women.

A growing body of research also shows that LGBTQ+ individuals can face significant discrimination in the workplace (Ragins, Singh, and Cornwell, 2007; Sears et al., 2021; DeSouza, Wesselmann, and Ispas, 2017). For example, Ragins, Singh, and Cornwell (2007) surveyed 534 individuals who identified as gay, lesbian, or bisexual about their workplace experiences. They found that 33.9 percent of respondents had experienced discrimination at work because of their sexual orientation and 37.2 percent had experienced discrimination at work because someone suspected they might be gay, lesbian, or bisexual. In addition, 10.5 percent had experienced physical harassment at work and 22.4 percent had experienced verbal harassment at work because of their sexual orientation. Experiences with discrimination influenced whether some respondents stayed at their jobs: 13.3 percent of respondents reported resign-

---

dent," while women may be described with words as "sympathetic" and "helpful." Heilman defines *prescriptive stereotypes* as stereotypes about "norms and behaviors that are suitable" for men and women (Heilman, 2001, pp. 658–659).

ing from a job as a result of being discriminated against because of their sexual orientation, 6.1 percent had been fired from a job because of their sexual orientation, and 11.4 percent reported leaving their previous job because they were discriminated against based on their sexual orientation.

Ragins, Singh, and Cornwell (2007) also found that concerns about being discriminated against shaped whether some respondents' were open about their sexual orientation at work, which, in turn, affected their mental health. Of those surveyed, 11.7 percent had not disclosed their sexual orientation to any of their colleagues at work, 37 percent had disclosed their sexual orientation to some but not all of their colleagues at work, 24.6 percent had disclosed their sexual orientation to most colleagues at work, and 26.77 percent had disclosed their sexual orientation to all of their colleagues at work. Those respondents who had not disclosed their sexual orientation to some or all of their colleagues experienced lower levels of career satisfaction, lower rates of job promotion, and higher levels of work-related stress and anxiety.

More recently, Sears et al. (2021) surveyed 935 individuals who identified as LGBT.[9] Of those surveyed, 45.5 percent said that they had experienced discrimination or harassment at work. Types of discrimination included being fired or not receiving a job offer. Types of harassment included verbal, physical, and sexual harassment. The authors also found that respondents believed it was necessary to take steps to avoid discrimination and harassment in the workplace. More than one-half of respondents also reported that they had not disclosed their LGBT identity to a supervisor, and almost 26 percent reported that they had not disclosed their LGBT identity to coworkers.

Neurodiversity Employment Literature

Emerging research is also examining hiring process biases that exclude neurodivergent individuals. We explored a body of literature seeking to define what it means to be neurodivergent, which identified some challenges that might be encountered by neurodivergent individuals during hiring processes and in the workplace and noted some of the ways that public- and private-sector organizations may be able to increase representation of neurodivergent employees that would add additional value to workforce populations.

Although there is not yet a clear definitional consensus about all types of populations that may constitute a neurodivergent workforce, there is recent convergence around the types of cognitive factors that could influence a future definition. EARN (undated) defines *neurodiversity* as the "natural way that people think, learn, perceive the world, interact and process information differently," and *neurodivergent* as populations that include "include autistic people; people with attention deficit hyperactivity disorder (ADHD), posttraumatic stress disorder (PTSD) and other mental health conditions; and people with learning disabilities." Furthermore, that "this group also includes people with other intellectual and developmental

---

[9] Sears et al., 2021, uses the term *LGBT* in their report, which differs from our use of *LGBTQ+*.

disabilities and a wide variety of conditions that can shape thinking, learning and perceiving the world" (EARN, undated).

The literature that we reviewed in this space identified challenges that might be encountered by neurodivergent individuals in the hiring process, and once employed. A *Harvard Business Review* article notes that the unemployment rate for a defined group of neurodivergent individuals (specifically those on the autism spectrum) in the United States reached 85 percent in 2020 (Praslova, 2021).[10] Loiacono and Ren (2018) reviewed hiring websites across 39 technology organizations across the Fortune 500 list for any information that listed accommodations for neurodiversity; although "most mentioned diversity in some way— either generally or in terms of gender, ethnicity, veterans, and LGBTQ specifically"—none of the sites "explicitly mentioned neurodiversity." Krzeminska et al. (2019) also are exploring ways to modify the Organizational Interventions Mitigating Individual Barriers framework to help hiring organizations construct new hiring process to accommodate an emerging neurodiverse workforce. JPMorgan Chase, Microsoft, SAP, and Hilton have started to recruit from the neurodiverse unemployment pool, and they have tailored job postings and the hiring and interview processes to accommodate neurodiverse populations.[11]

We also reviewed a small sample of studies and articles that highlighted several recent workplace hiring practices (e.g., recruitment, interviews, screening) that may positively affected neurodivergent individuals in the future (Khan et al., 2022; Sumner and Brown, 2015).[12] There have also been various pilot programs undertaken at private companies to study how some neurodivergent groups of employees work, including programs and studies focused on employees on the autism spectrum that have found that such employees can be more productive than their neurotypical counterparts, specifically in accomplishing detailed work involving pattern recognition, sustained focus, and complex information-processing (Heckenberg and Berman, 2021; Caminiti, 2022). Numerous organizations throughout the private sector are modifying hiring assessments and interview structure to be inclusive of neurodivergent individuals (e.g., removing résumé and interview requirements in lieu of short online assessments) and, in some cases, creating entire staffing services made up of neurodiverse individuals, particularly with the types of emerging skill sets (e.g., data science, cybersecurity) that the U.S. government historically has struggled to attract, hire, and retain (Manson, 2022; Morris, Begel, and Wiedermann, 2015).[13]

---

[10] Note that the author also noted that "50% of managers surveyed in the U.K. admitted they would not hire neurodivergent candidates" (Praslova, 2021).

[11] For example, JPMorgan Chase has adapted job postings that discount the need for verbal communication. Microsoft has also instituted a four-day hiring and interview process that includes virtual interview options and team-building exercises to ease candidate anxiety (Caminiti, 2022).

[12] See, for example, Khan et al., 2022; and Sumner and Brown, 2015, p. 77.

[13] A Bloomberg article notes that neurodiverse individuals are becoming especially useful within artificial intelligence context (e.g., programming and analysis), which can benefit from viewpoints that differ from nondivergent (neurotypical) individuals (Manson, 2022; Morris, Begel, and Wiedermann, 2015).

The U.S. government has been looking for ways to increase its access to new talent, including neurodivergent individuals (Ford and Shukla, 2022; Ogrysko, 2021. Military components are seeking to diversify active duty forces through increased neurodivergent representation (Davis, 2021). The National Geospatial-Intelligence Agency (NGA) is investing in a program to develop a Neurodiverse Federal Workforce (NFW) Pilot Program, which seeks to modernize how "neurodivergent job candidates are recruited, hired, and retained for federal positions" toward creating a more "neurodiverse federal workforce (NFW)" (NGA, 2021; OPM, 2022).[14] Results from the NFW Pilot will culminate in the creation of a playbook that will assist U.S. government departments and agencies develop and implement future pilot programs to fill critical workforce needs. The U.S. Department of Labor is also seeking to diversify a more neurodivergent workforce across the U.S. government and has cited the playbook to showcase the value of neurodiversity for departments and agencies seeking to implement similar programs (U.S. Department of Labor, Office of Disability Employment Office, 2021).

Summary

Our literature review suggests that there is a basis for concern about the potential for bias, discrimination, and sources of inequity based on race or ethnicity, gender, gender identity, sexual orientation, or neurodivergence. Research related to different areas of employment shows that people of color face significant obstacles when seeking jobs. These obstacles include structural factors and instances of individual-level racial discrimination that may serve as mechanisms of exclusion. Previous research also reveals persistent obstacles in the workplace for women, LGBTQ+ individuals, and neurodivergent individuals.[15] These findings are informative for our understanding of the potential for bias and sources of inequity in the security clearance process because they reveal factors that *may* have a negative or disproportionate impact on applicants from diverse backgrounds and that could present barriers as applicants traverse the structural and human elements of the personnel vetting process.

---

[14] NGA contracted with the MITRE Corporation to initiate this NFW Pilot in December 2021 that is intended to "function as a single solution to address two issues: disproportionate unemployment in the autism community and a high demand for qualified federal tech talent." For more information, see Thomas, 2021; and NGA, 2021.

[15] It is important to emphasize that categories of exclusion can intersect to further affect the experiences of members of marginalized groups. Focusing specifically on the experiences of Black women, Crenshaw (2013) argues that it is important to consider race and gender when seeking to unpacking the dynamics of oppression. Research has consistently shown that discrimination can be shaped by multiple factors, such as race, gender, and LGBTQ+ status. For example, the Williams Institute's report on workplace discrimination and LGBT individuals found that LGBT people of color were more likely than White LGBT individuals to report experiencing discrimination and harassment at work (Sears et al., 2021). In addition, the report found that transgender individuals were more likely to report experiencing workplace discrimination than cisgender individuals.

CHAPTER 3

Observations and Themes from Discussions with Personnel Vetting and DEIA Experts

This chapter discusses observations and themes gained from semistructured discussions with current and former U.S. government personnel vetting experts and practitioners and both U.S. government and private-sector DEIA experts. In these conversations, we asked about elements in the personnel vetting process that have the potential to contribute to racial or other bias and inequity (focusing on race or ethnicity, gender, gender identity, sexual orientation, and neurodiversity); any ongoing DEIA-related initiatives or training, particularly those related to the vetting process; and any other relevant information that discussants were aware of on the topic. We centered these discussions on the structural and human elements of the security clearance personnel vetting process. For the structural element of the process, we focused on

- the questionnaire that candidates and staff are asked to fill out (SF-86), which is ultimately submitted to an investigator to validate and pursue potential leads of information related to risk factors
- the security clearance adjudicative guidelines (SEAD-4), which identify risk factors that an individual may present and provides the basis on which the government assesses and adjudicates an individual.

For the human element of the process, we focused on how perceptions and judgments of the investigators, adjudicators, and quality reviewers may have the potential to affect the outcome of the process. Finally, we asked discussants about any suggestions on areas for improvement to address the potential for biases and inequities in the personnel vetting process.

Approach and Methods

We identified 28 potential discussants with either DEIA or personnel vetting backgrounds who were suggested by the PAC PMO sponsor, were contacts within the study team's professional network, or were recommended using snowball-sampling suggestions of additional experts from our participants. Appendix C provides an anonymized summary list of discussants and the semistructured protocol guides used for the discussions.

We conducted 18 discussions with a total of 20 discussants from August 2022 to late October 2022. Our final discussant sample consisted of 12 U.S. government personnel vetting SMEs and eight DEIA SMEs. This group was not a representative or generalizable population sample, but the discussions provide useful insights from individuals who are experts in the two key functional subject areas related to this study topic. Discussions were conducted at the unclassified level, with no discussions video or audio recorded.

We took detailed notes during the discussions, and, using those, we conducted a qualitative manual curation of the notes to find general themes and observations across them and to identify any outlier perspectives. In parallel, we also used Dedoose coding software for our analysis.[1] We created a coding scheme consisting of 93 codes related to perceptions of bias in the hiring, background investigation, and adjudicative SSC phases; comments on the SF-86; comments on the adjudicative guidelines; comments on cultural or bias training; recommendations to reduce bias; perceptions of support for DEIA efforts; and other important reflections. Our coding scheme can be found in Appendix D.

We organized our thematic analysis through Dedoose around excerpts tagged with codes focused on the presence or absence of bias and the degree to which respondents noticed bias (e.g., "Racial bias exists in hiring phase"; "Respondent has not noticed neurodiversity bias in background investigation phase"; "Gender bias does not exist in adjudicative phase"). We binned areas for improvement to address potential for bias or inequity that were offered by the discussants.

Limitations

Some research indicates that there is the potential for research respondents to be affected by "social desirability bias," which means that some respondents may respond to questions in ways that they believe are most socially desirable (Bergen and Labonté, 2020). Although we expressed to all discussants that we sought out their candid responses and observations regarding the topics discussed, the possibility for some social desirability bias remains. For example, in this study, some respondents may have been less likely to express negative views about ongoing DEIA initiatives because of perceptions that it may not be what is socially desirable, or they knew the focus of this study was to explore the potential for bias and sources of inequity in the personnel vetting process. To try and reduce the impact of this type of bias, our discussions were conducted with multiple researchers participating in each session from a variety of backgrounds. This factor reduced the chance that respondents' views were consistently shaped by interactions with one team member. In addition, we conducted the discussions with respondents in a variety of positions and with different backgrounds to ensure that we gathered a broader set of perspectives and experiences. However, social desirability

---

[1] Dedoose (undated) is a qualitative data analysis software program that allows for systematic coding of qualitative data, including interview transcripts.

bias could have still affected how some respondents talked about DEIA or the potential for bias and inequity, and that our overall results may not fully reflect the degree and potential variety of views and experiences related to this topic.

The Structural Element

The SF-86 is the written questionnaire by which an individual provides requested information related to the SEAD-4 guidelines to inform the investigation and adjudication of their security clearance eligibility. SEAD-4 (2017) provides the single common adjudicative criteria for making a security clearance eligibility determination; its 13 adjudicative guidelines are the basis on which several variables in an individual's life are assessed to decide whether the individual is an acceptable security risk. Taken together, these form the core structure of the personnel vetting background investigation and security clearance adjudication process. We spoke to personnel vetting SMEs and DEIA SMEs about both the SF-86 form and the SEAD-4 guidelines to help identify any areas that, given their experience and expertise, (1) might reveal information about an individual's race or ethnicity, gender, gender identity, sexual orientation, or neurodivergence and/or (2) might present concerns when it comes to potential bias and inequity in the process. What follows are observations and themes from those discussions.

General Discussant Observations

Regarding the identification of areas where the structure of the process might present concerns when it comes to potential bias and inequity, several personnel vetting discussants commented that the structure of the personnel vetting process is intended to be objective regardless of an individual's demographic background. One discussant remarked that although they do not view any single section or question of the SF-86 to be intentionally biased, the form as a whole "does not seem like it was designed to be inclusive."[2] Rather, the individual suggested that the form (and the structure of the security clearance process) appears tailored to favor for adjudication of an "Anglo-Saxon, heterosexual candidate" who has lived in the same place, not traveled overseas, and held the same occupational position for a decade.[3] Such an applicant is likely to have fewer potential reportable items that SEAD-4 suggests could present a national security risk and, therefore, fewer triggers to require additional investigatory follow-up and mitigation considerations. A few discussants offered comments that the process was not created to be inclusive; the purpose of the process is to be discerning in identifying candidates who are trustworthy to protect national security, but also to screen out those who present an unacceptable national security risk based on certain standards and to deny

---

[2] See Discussant ID 21 in Table C.1.

[3] See Discussant ID 21 in Table C.1.

them security clearance eligibility based on that assessed risk. Another discussant asserted that "there are multiple places in the SF-86 where the language is exclusionary"[4]—including with regard to identification of sex (as binary male/female) and also language in the mental health section—and the exclusionary language presents barriers for a more diverse and equitable applicant set entering the cleared workforce. This discussant expressed the concern that individuals might be dissuaded from even applying to a position because of exclusionary language in the form.

Race and Ethnicity

Information on race and ethnicity is not collected explicitly as a category or structural requirement in the SF-86 form, but several discussants pointed out that it is often knowable or at least likely to be assumed. This information can be based on a person's name, where they have lived (whether in the United States or abroad and what races and ethnicities may live predominantly in that location), what foreign contacts they have declared, and/or what familial connections they may have reported outside the United States. Knowing that information could ultimately affect the perceptions of an investigator or adjudicator about the individual, based on assumed race or ethnicity. Along those lines, one discussant said, "There's a potential for bias, like for anything based on names . . . with respect to ethnic or naturalized citizens because there's more to look at for their background investigation and more potential for disqualifying information that's subjective."[5]

Related to both the SF-86 and SEAD-4 guidelines, several of our discussants pointed out that knowing where a person lived and went to school could reveal information about race and ethnicity. One personnel vetting discussant described that there is potential for racial bias from criminal history record reporting or the criminal record (related to Guideline J–Criminal Conduct) in the investigative process, as it relates to where a candidate's city of residence. Specifically the discussant said "that police record, what city it's in, could have an impact."[6] For example, a candidate from a small rural town who has drug use on their criminal record (related to Guideline H–Drug Involvement) may be seen by an investigator or adjudicator as exhibiting "youthful exuberance," while the discussant said an urban-dwelling candidate with a similar record "that's gonna be a threat"[7] and, therefore, is likely to trigger additional investigation into their background. Both examples have the same overall risk behavior of concern regarding drug use, but the follow-up and investigative tail into each may not be equal.

A few discussants pointed out that foreign business and professional affiliations can be revealing about an individual's race or ethnicity. Similarly, foreign contacts and familial

---

[4]   See Discussant ID 1 in Table C.1.

[5]   See Discussant ID 4 in Table C.1.

[6]   See Discussant ID 16 in Table C.1.

[7]   See Discussant ID 16 in Table C.1.

affiliations (both related to Guideline B–Foreign Influence) listed on the SF-86 could be a potential pointer to an individual's race or ethnicity and could lead to different treatment as a result. For example, one discussant mentioned that "if you have an undocumented family member, you're automatically some sort of risk"[8] with the SEAD-4 guidelines, requiring additional investigation per the investigative requirements, but commented that problematic because that individual may get an additional level of scrutiny when they, as the applicant, may not actually present any concerning risk.

Gender, Gender Identity, or Sexual Orientation

Unlike race or ethnicity, an individual's sex is a required data category (with a box to check either "male" or "female") on the SF-86, so investigators and adjudicators know that piece of information from the start about the individual that they are investigating or adjudicating. As a few discussants pointed out, the form requires the individual to list other names used, including maiden names. Therefore, an investigator or adjudicator would know whether the individual identifies as a male or female, and whether the individual is or has been married and had a name change associated with that marriage.

Two discussants pointed out that the necessary provision of a candidate's employment history in the SF-86 can also reveal information about whether a candidate chose to be a stay-at-home parent or worked reduced hours. This provision could be most problematic for the potential bias or sources of inequity for women, because women (most commonly) take on caregiving roles and have subsequent perceived unexplained gaps or reduced hours in employment.

A few of our discussants also pointed out that investigators and adjudicators might also be able to infer or assume an individual's sexual orientation or same-sex marriage by combining the sex that the individual identified in the form and the perceived sex of the spouse or partner listed in the section of the SF-86 because a spouse's name is required to be provided. Several discussants pointed out that Guideline D—which specifically considers types of sexual behavior that may be a security concern—is one of the most difficult to assess objectively. Guideline D does specify that "sexual orientation or preference may not be used as a basis for or a disqualifying factor in determining a person's eligibility for a security clearance," but the concern expressed by the discussants was that adjudicating this guideline includes a level of subjective judgment on what activity may be considered subject to "coercion, exploitation, duress, or reflects lack of judgment or discretion" per the Guideline D language (Office of the Director of Intelligence, 2017). One personnel vetting SME expressed that this is an area where individuals—because of sexual preferences—may "feel like they have to be dishonest or if they're honest they'll feel it will disqualify."[9]

---

[8] See Discussant ID 21 in Table C.1.

[9] See Discussant ID 13 in Table C.1.

Related to gender identity, the SF-86 does not allow for any other answer other than male/female identifiers. So, this factor further complicates filling out the form for a person who may identify as a different gender other than their birth sex—information that could have a significant chance of being revealed in the investigative process. One discussant informed us that they have had individuals apply for a vetted position who have reached out to express concerns about being transsexual, giving one example where an individual said, "I happen to be trans; I have to provide prior names used and I am uncomfortable having to out myself."[10] Several discussants also pointed out that the SF-86 form asks, "Were you born a male after December 31, 1959?" to determine whether the individual registered for the Selective Service, as required. If an individual answers "yes" to that question but now identifies in the questionnaire as a female, such a transgender or transitioned candidate could potentially out themselves in the security clearance process to the investigator and/or adjudicator when they may not have even shared that personal information with family, friends, or employers. One discussant suggested that having questions such as these (which could inadvertently reveal an individual's gender identity before they are ready to so) without a clear understanding of "why they have to access this and who has access to the information"[11] and how that information will be used or shared could also have a chilling effect for certain candidates even completing the questionnaire. Additionally, the discussant pointed out that the SF-86 uses binary language to identify brother-sister relationships and mother-father relationships—in addition to asking for their names—which can also reveal information about individuals' gender identities who are not even themselves the subjects of the security clearance process.

Neurodiversity

There is no structural requirement in the SF-86 form for a neurodivergent individual to declare their neurodivergence or a disability, but some of the answers the person provides in the form may reveal that they are part of the neurodivergent population. For example, two of our discussants mentioned that the mental health questions (related to Guideline I–Emotional, Mental, and Personality Disorders) may end up revealing information about an individual who has ADHD or an individual with autism, who has sought out therapy or counseling. Another discussant said that with the SF-86, "one issue is mental health—and the way it's mentioned it contradicts the accessibility piece"[12] and can have the impact of seeming noninclusive for applicants.

Additionally, two discussants mentioned that if an individual has attended a school tailored to their specific learning needs, the school would be listed in the SF-86 section titled "Where you Went to School" and could provide revelatory information about the individual's neurodivergence. One DEIA SME discussant said that it is not uncommon for some neurodi-

---

[10] See Discussant ID 2 in Table C.1.

[11] See Discussant ID 2 in Table C.1.

[12] See Discussant ID 1 in Table C.1.

vergent individuals to have "shuffled around a lot and had a lot of unemployment," [13] or have only retained employment for a month or so; that information would be documented in the "Employment Activities" section of the SF-86.

Related to potential inequities in the process, two DEIA SME discussants with experience working with neurodivergent individuals pointed out that the way the questions of the SF-86 form are phrased could be particularly challenging for some neurodivergent individuals to answer, because some neurodivergent candidates may be more absolute and literal in what they are being asked and how they are answering. One DEIA SME discussant explained further that some neurodivergent individuals who are asked to answer whether they have "close and continuing" contacts (related to Guideline B–Foreign Influence), may want to understand what exactly that means and how precisely that is defined before answering; for some neurodivergent individuals, ambiguous questions like those are problematic.[14]

Another discussant gave an example of a challenge that a neurodivergent individual may encounter before the personnel vetting process even begins, related to accessibility issues with the USAJOBS website. The platform indicates on job announcements that if accommodations are needed to complete the application (e.g., use of a proxy, extra time to complete, sending a hard copy of forms in large print), that the candidate should connect with the provided contact (USAJOBS, undated). However, the discussant observed that

> nowhere on USAJOBS makes it clear to applicants how to ask for accommodations and that they'll be provided quickly. Usually on a job announcement it says "If you need accommodations, contact whomever," who may or may not be able to respond if the job closes that day.[15]

This aspect could result in the job posting window for a cleared position closing before an interested neurodivergent candidate gets the opportunity to have appropriate accommodations arranged to apply in time.

The Human Element

In addition to the structure of the security clearance process, we also examined how potential perceptions and judgments in the human elements of the process—including the investigators, the adjudicators, and the quality reviewers—could allow for potential bias or inequity in the outcome of the process. We spoke to personnel vetting and DEIA SMEs regarding what they have observed related to the human element of the process to help identify any areas that, given their experience and expertise, might reveal where bias/inequity has been or could

---

[13] See Discussant ID 15 in Table C.1.

[14] See Discussant ID 17 in Table C.1.

[15] See Discussant ID 19 in Table C.1.

be introduced in the process, in particular related to individual's race or ethnicity, gender, gender identity, sexual orientation, or neurodivergence. What follows are observations and themes from those discussions.

General Discussant Observations

Most discussants emphasized that there are standards that are applied throughout the personnel vetting process to ensure as much objectivity as possible. As one discussant put it, the process is intended not to be geared toward "anything other than what does this background indicate and how we make a decision based on character, conduct, and attitudes toward behavior and crossing our t's through multiple levels of review."[16] However, most discussants also acknowledged that there is the potential for individual cases of bias or sources of inequity based on the human interactions and human judgment that is a required part of the hiring, investigative, and adjudicative processes. As one discussant expressed, "unintentional bias can reshape things in interviews" being conducted as part of the investigation process with people from different communities.[17] Another discussant said, "when we think about bias, it may not be just in the process itself, but some of those adjudicators may have bias,"[18] which could result in bias and sources of inequity for a candidate.

Several personnel vetting SMEs reported that they had never personally witnessed bias related to race, gender, gender identity, sexual orientation, or neurodivergence in the SSC process, but they acknowledged the potential for bias to occur. One personnel vetting SME believed strongly that there is no bias related to these categories in either the investigative or adjudicative processes, pointing to the fact that they have seen no data that support that such bias exists. A few discussants emphasized there are checks and balances and oversight mechanisms within the system to help mitigate any potential for bias or inequity.

One personnel vetting SME said there is "definitely bias out there on the investigator side,"[19] though went on to say that this may be unintentional bias, because the investigators are humans with their own backgrounds and experiences who are collecting information and then they are writing the report that goes to adjudication, and those investigators are ultimately deciding what that adjudicator sees. Another personnel vetting SME said that although they could not point to a case where they knew that bias played a role in the adjudication of eligibility, they did think that it happens after hearing the informal chatter of colleagues saying such things as "as soon as I saw that name" or "as soon as I saw where they had visited, how many children they had, I knew they wouldn't get cleared."[20] This SME

---

[16] See Discussant ID 4 in Table C.1.

[17] See Discussant ID 7 in Table C.1.

[18] See Discussant ID 1 in Table C.1.

[19] See Discussant ID 9 in Table C.1.

[20] See Discussant ID 16 in Table C.1.

commented that at the core of the issue is stereotypes—acknowledging they are a part of the human element, and that it is not easy to separate that in every situation and apply the guidelines objectively.

One personnel vetting SME emphasized that the system in place recognizes how the human element affects the process, and some of the training that is provided to investigators is supposed to help them to be more conversational—and less automated—when interacting with individuals as part of the investigative process. However, this can also mean that individuals can deviate from the parameters of what is an appropriate question if they do not know better. One example given by this discussant (which happened in the training environment, so it could be corrected) was an investigator's attempt at trying to elicit information related to Guideline D (the sexual behavior guideline); the investigator improvised a question, asking, "Did you ever enter a ladies bathroom?"[21] The personnel vetting SME emphasized that what was assessed to be an inappropriate question could be addressed because it occurred during training—however, if a question like this was asked in the course of an investigation, it would be very uncomfortable for the applicant, and they would likely be concerned why the investigator was asking such a question, even if there may have been no malicious intent. The SME also pointed out that if an investigator asks a question like that every time, it is possible that they would be reported by an applicant at some point for asking inappropriate questions in the interview; if so, at a minimum this would generally result in supervisory counseling of the investigator. However, there is also the possibility that inappropriate questioning like this could occur and never be reported by the subjects of the interviews.

Several personnel vetting SMEs emphasized that there are checks and balances built into the system. For example, there are quality reviewers who are looking at sets of investigative packages and sets of adjudicative decisions to ensure that the process and decisions were in keeping with the guidelines and were appropriately made. Two personnel vetting SMEs noted that they believe that a second or even third level of quality review has helped decrease the potential for bias and inequity in the adjudication phase. A few personnel vetting SME discussants spoke about "check rides" that are done with the agents to observe how they are conducting their interviews and engagements with subjects and other individuals being interviewed, so if there is anything done outside the handbook or policies/procedures, the investigator receives feedback on how to improve.

Race and Ethnicity

None of our discussants reported that they had been directly involved in vetting cases in which they knew that racial or ethnic bias influenced the outcome and resulted in a negative adjudicative decision for eligibility. However, many discussants confirmed that the human element of the process could allow for potential inequity or bias if an investigator or adjudicator held biases regarding an individual's race or ethnicity and treated the applicant's case

---

[21] See Discussant ID 6 in Table C.1.

differently as a result. Some discussants provided examples where they either witnessed or had heard about problematic behavior or comments related to race and ethnicity by personnel involved in the vetting process.

Several discussants pointed out that assessing the Guideline B–Foreign Influence can be particularly rife with the potential for racial or ethnic bias and inequity in the experience of an applicant in the process. One personnel vetting SME said "foreign influence, that's another one depending on whether the person has family members, foreign contacts that come to visit . . . and not judging someone coming from Australia so differently versus someone from Mexico."[22] Another discussant pointed out that when it comes to ethnicity and assessing risk, sometimes investigators are required to dig deeper to understand whether the individual's ties to a foreign country present an unacceptable national security risk, but the discussant commented that bias can manifest itself in the form of

> extra scrutiny based on ethnicity or where the family came from or whatever the hotspot is at the time . . . so you [as an investigator] can choose to go through normal questioning and do follow-up, but sometimes you might steer into extra things when that wasn't the point and wasn't warranted.[23]

One discussant gave an example of an investigator who got reported and later counseled for inappropriate conduct because the investigator was "mistreating people based on their accent",[24] specifically, when the investigator could not understand the interviewee, they talked over them, cut them off, and laughed at the interviewee—and this was an interview of a third-party individual, not the candidate themselves. This discussant explained that such behavior would not necessarily show up in an investigator's write up—they can tell you the questions they asked, and the answer from the interviewee, but may not convey in their report how they responded to the answer and how they treated the individual as part of the investigation process.

A different discussant reflected on an instance where they were on a ride-along during which they witnessed an investigator doing "overwork" on a case in which the investigator reportedly spent an extra hour unnecessarily drilling into details about the candidate's background, including questions that are not normally asked. Our SME believed this "overwork" was unwarranted and was done based on assumptions about the candidate's ethnic background, saying there was a point where, if the discussant were the subject, the discussant would feel like "are they attacking me because my family is not originally from the [United States], or my skin is dark so are you assuming I did something more than just smoke marijuana?"[25] A discussant pointed out that quality reviewers can review "thousands of

---

[22] See Discussant ID 16 in Table C.1.

[23] See Discussant ID 8 in Table C.1.

[24] See Discussant ID 13 in Table C.1.

[25] See Discussant ID 8 in Table C.1.

cases, and sometimes you can tell [the investigator] didn't need to ask that question, or put it in the report,"[26] which the discussant said then raises the question of how many times are inappropriate questions being asked and not put in a report (and thus not reviewed). A discussant shared that there was one case in which an individual made it as far as the polygraph phase, and a polygrapher drilled down on the fact that the individual attended a racial justice protest. This "left the individual the impression that the polygrapher was accusing [them] of unlawful activity" when the applicant believed they were just exercising a First Amendment right; that individual dropped out of the process because of that experience.[27]

A few SMEs pointed out that they do believe that certain assumptions and biases arise when it comes to drug use, with some individuals factoring in stereotypes about particular groups. Similarly some discussants raised the potential for criminal history records information, combined with information about where someone is from in the United States, could contribute to stereotypes and bias. One discussant said that if "someone has a rap sheet the size of your arm . . . there is an opportunity for someone to be biased and maybe not necessarily report that way but feel that way, saying 'well they shouldn't have a clearance'"; the discussant made clear they had not seen this in any official metrics or reports, but "very much so believe that it happens."[28] Another discussant made the comment that an address says the exact community an applicant is from and can reveal socioeconomic status, explaining that "there are biases that live in [an] address and if you know you have to go out there" to an address that may be perceived as a "tough area," then "it compounds those biases as you visit those areas."[29]

Gender, Gender Identity, and Sexual Orientation

None of our discussants reported that they had been directly involved in vetting cases where they knew that gender, gender identity, or sexual orientation bias influenced the outcome and resulted in a negative adjudicative decision for eligibility. However, several discussants confirmed that the human judgment aspects of the process could allow for the potential inequity or bias in the way an individual was perceived or experienced the process, in particular if an investigator or adjudicator held biases regarding a particular gender or LGBTQ+ individuals and thus treated the applicant's case differently.

Several personnel vetting discussants confirmed that in the course of an investigation and adjudication, an individual's sex (as declared on the SF-86) is known, and that an individual's gender identity or sexual orientation may become known. Also, as standard investigatory practice, certain pieces of information provided in the SF-86 are confirmed with the applicant. Although an individual's sex is a piece of information required in the form, one

---

[26] See Discussant ID 8 in Table C.1.

[27] See Discussant ID 11 in Table C.1.

[28] See Discussant ID 9 in Table C.1.

[29] See Discussant ID 13 in Table C.1.

discussant pointed out that investigators are not trained to verify an individual's sex with the applicant directly or to verify the physical information they are asked to provide on the form; however, it would likely be noticeable if an individual's physical appearance (or perceived gender) did not match the sex declared on the form.

Relatedly, a discussant confirmed that the Selected Service question in the SF-86 ("Were you born a male after December 31, 1959?") has caused problems in the course of the verification process (in part because it can reveal an individual's gender identity being different then their identified sex on the form), so much so that investigators have "gone to not even asking that question anymore" for verification purposes.[30] Another discussant pointed out that investigators tend to use binary terms in their engagements with individuals, in part because there is not training to be culturally sensitive or aware otherwise; the discussant expressed the view that "field investigators have to move away from a binary way of thinking" to be more inclusive of the population who may be applying for these positions.[31]

Regarding the potential to know an individual's sexual orientation, another personnel vetting discussant confirmed "on the [SF-] 86 you have to list your spouse . . . if the subject is a female and then they list a female name then you can assume it's likely a same-sex marriage or cohabitant."[32] As far as addressing Guideline D–Sexual Behavior as a potential issue in the course of an investigation and adjudication, one discussant indicated "a lot of the information, especially those who are not in a mainstream ideal . . . we don't know if they think that is deviant to us. And that is the key thing"[33] that is being assessed when it comes to Guideline D. This discussant pointed out that, historically, same-sex relationships were considered problematic in some prior versions of adjudicative guidelines, but that has changed and now Guideline D makes explicit that "sexual orientation or preference may not be used as a basis for or cannot be basis of disqualifying factor" (Director of Central Intelligence Directive No. 1/14 and Annex A Adjudication Guidelines, 1976; Office of the Director of Intelligence, 2017). The discussant went on to say that an individual going through the process may well know that the guideline related to sexual behavior has changed, but think that "historical data will tell me you used it against people like me."[34] Another discussant keyed in on how loosely problematic sexual behavior is defined in Guideline D, and said that leaves room for considerable interpretation and subjectivity by an investigator and adjudicator. The discussant expressed that

---

[30] See Discussant ID 6 in Table C.1.

[31] See Discussant ID 7 in Table C.1.

[32] See Discussant ID 26 in Table C.1.

[33] See Discussant ID 13 in Table C.1.

[34] See Discussant ID 13 in Table C.1.

the sexual behavior guideline is the one that really keys in because what is the purpose of it? We were always told is there potential for blackmail and I get that but . . . that whole area is uncomfortable to know what to ask if you haven't been a part of that.[35]

Regarding the difficultly of objectively assessing the sexual behavior guideline, another discussant said "the sexual behavior question is—I will tell you, we struggle with that."[36] One discussant gave an example of this, citing a case study in a personnel vetting training module that is focused on objectivity with regard to favorable and unfavorable bias. The case study was described as being "about a cross-dresser" who has a second job at a "cabaret club"; the point of the case is not to deny the individual because of how they dress, but because they did not disclose a second job as required. Trainees tended to want to disqualify because of sexual behavior, as opposed to because the individual lied on the form; however, the case was supposed to be denied based on personal conduct related to the lying, and not sexual behavior.[37]

Neurodiversity

None of our discussants reported that they had been directly involved in vetting cases where they knew that an individual's neurodivergence influenced the outcome and resulted in a negative adjudicative decision for eligibility. However, a few discussants shared their perspectives that the human element of the process could allow for the potential of inequity or bias in the way a neurodivergent individual is perceived or experiences the process, largely because of potential assumptions about on mental health and perceived abnormal behaviors.

One DEIA SME discussant indicated that "[many] people in neurodivergent communities have worked with some kind of counselor and have had some kind of mental health diagnosis" at some point in their lives,[38] which could come up in the background investigation, although the discussants recognized mental health treatment is something that the government has tried to encourage for those who need it, as a proactive measure to seek help. Additionally, another DEIA SME discussant pointed out the subjective nature of Guideline I— which states that "emotional, mental, and personality disorders . . . are a security concern because they may indicate a defect in judgment, reliability, or stability" (Office of the Director of National Intelligence, 2017)—relies on the adjudicator to make a judgment on whether a neurodivergent individual (who may have been diagnosed with a "disorder" of concern) "might have such a 'defect.'"[39] One of our DEIA SME discussants said they know of a neurodivergent individual who went through the security clearance process and did not pass; they

---

[35] See Discussant ID 6 in Table C.1.

[36] See Discussant ID 21 in Table C.1.

[37] See Discussant ID 22 in Table C.1.

[38] See Discussant ID 15 in Table C.1.

[39] See Discussant ID 17 in Table C.1.

put in multiple requests to find out why exactly they did not pass, but the individual is "pretty sure it's mental health issues in the past."[40]

Several discussants pointed out that some neurodivergent individuals may behave and present themselves differently than neurotypical individuals. One discussant pointed out that certain developmental disabilities and/or neurodivergent characteristics could affect "how someone would conduct themselves in public, management of finances and use of alcohol and drugs"[41] and said those are areas that may need to receive appropriate consideration, when evaluating a neurodivergent individual's background check. Two DEIA SME discussants expressed the concern that the interview requirement (and for some agencies, the polygraph requirement) can be uneven for some neurodivergent individuals—and more problematic than for most neurotypical individuals.[42] One discussant indicated that some neurodivergent individuals can come across differently (and potentially suspiciously for those who avoid eye contact, look around, fidget, and are visibly uncomfortable) to an interviewer. According to this discussant, "Some individuals give very long and wholesome answers because they want to give the right answer. Others can be very dry and to the point."[43] Another discussant pointed out that an investigator understanding these varied communication styles is a "huge thing because some neurodiverse individuals don't know how they come off."[44] The combination of what some neurodivergent individuals say—and how they say it—could lead to assumptions about trustworthiness and reliability that could have an adverse outcome on a security clearance determination.

Potential Areas for Improvement

After discussions about the structural and human elements of the security clearance process, we asked discussants about any suggestions for areas for improvement to address the potential for biases and sources of inequity in the personnel vetting process. Most of the issues raised by discussants fell into three areas: (1) concerns about the structural forms and guidelines that shape the process to address potential areas of bias or inequity, (2) lack of training

---

[40] See Discussant ID 15 in Table C.1.

[41] See Discussant ID 19 in Table C.1.

[42] For example, recent RAND research noted that,

> The clearance process is designed for neurotypical candidates who can complete large amounts of complex paperwork, answer questions directly and promptly, make eye contact, and communicate without fidgeting. Interview participants in the study—including a former polygraph examiner—said they worried about how many candidates do not pass the process because their behavior is considered "suspicious and untrustworthy" simply because it does not fall within the range of expected behavior." (Weinbaum et al., 2023)

For a discussion of neurodiversity and polygraph use, see Fordham University, School of Law, 2020.

[43] See Discussant ID 17 in Table C.1.

[44] See Discussant ID 15 in Table C.1.

related to cultural sensitivity and related bias for those involved in the personnel vetting process, and (3) lack of collection and analysis of demographic information to understand whether and where bias and inequity might be occurring in the process.

Forms and Guidelines

In the structural element part of this chapter, we summarized areas where discussants pointed to certain sections of the SF-86 and language in the adjudicative guidelines that might be problematic when considering the potential for bias or inequity. Some discussants recommended that those documents be reviewed to see whether revisions are warranted. Regarding the structural process as a whole, one discussant stated that "overall, the purpose of doing this and taking down barriers to opportunity and looking at how the standard process, even with its need and place, but how it eliminates so many talented people that are needed by doing it that way."[45]

Several discussants suggested that the SF-86 should be reviewed to ensure that the information it is collecting and how it is asking for that information (e.g., with regard to sex, gender identity, mental health) are necessary and appropriate to ultimately adjudicate the level of risk that an individual presents. One discussant thought that "sex and gender should be removed from the SF-86,"[46] in part because it has limited utility now as a data point to verify an individual's identity, given the widespread ability for individuals across the United States to legally change their gender identity. Two other discussants recommended that the SF-86 form be reviewed to ensure that it is as simple and clear as possible for all applicants to understand what is being asked, which will also serve the purpose of helping neurodivergent individuals to also comprehend better how to answer those questions.[47] One discussant also recommended "clarity either on form itself and/or with investigators communicating with applicants about why we have to collect prior names or for other questions . . . and who the data is shared with"[48] to increase comprehension by applicants on why the information is being asked and how it will be used. As mentioned earlier, another discussant recommended revising the mental health section of the SF-86, indicating that the way it is phrased now contradicts the accessibility piece of the objectives of DEIA.

Some discussants pointed to the need for the SEAD-4 Adjudicative Guidelines to be reviewed as well to identify areas where language might be problematic in judging individuals inequitably who have diverse racial, ethnic, gender identity, sexual orientation, or neurodivergent backgrounds. One discussant suggested that "bias could arise in any of these

---

[45] See Discussant ID 15 in Table C.1.

[46] See Discussant ID 2 in Table C.1.

[47] See Discussant ID 15 and Discussant ID 17 in Table C.1.

[48] See Discussant ID 2 in Table C.1.

categories"[49] of the SEAD-4 guidelines. Multiple other discussants pointed to Guideline D–Sexual Behavior as one that needed review and clarification because it is one of the most difficult for adjudicators to assess objectively and consistently, as written currently. Several discussants pointed to Guideline I–Emotional, Mental, and Personality Disorders as one worth reviewing and potentially revising to add clarity regarding specific behaviors or diagnoses that present a possible security concern.

Training/Awareness and Institutionalization

Many of our discussants indicated that they had participated in basic or introductory training on implicit bias or DEIA-related training as part of their onboarding and/or ongoing professional development at their agencies, but none of that training was tailored specifically to the personnel vetting process. One discussant confirmed that adjudicators go through training modules related to objectivity, and how to be aware of favorable and unfavorable cognitive bias, and another discussant affirmed that adjudicators are subject to required professional certification. However, one discussant spoke about investigative training and said "since training is so infrequent, our investigators mostly learn from what comes back from supervisor or review."[50] Regarding cultural sensitivity and bias training, one discussant said, "We haven't identified any issues that relate to that, so we haven't prioritized any training to that."[51] A different discussant said, "I don't know of any good training, there are just the 101s."[52] Another discussant said they believed there is "not currently a DEIA training much less gender inclusivity for investigators and adjudicators . . . so there is opportunity and necessity."[53]

Not every discussant felt that tailored training on cultural competence or bias/inequity related topics is warranted. One discussant said,

> The amount of folks that identify in any of these categories, even as being gay, these are obviously changing demographics in age and population of American culture but still relatively small in percentage. So the idea of putting a lot of training resources into what may or may not be a problem for a population that is arguably very small for the general population is one that bears additional scrutiny.[54]

However, many of our discussants indicated that they either thought it would be helpful or saw a need for cultural competence training, and training that addresses potential for bias

---

[49] See Discussant ID 9 in Table C.1.

[50] See Discussant ID 21 in Table C.1.

[51] See Discussant ID 4 in Table C.1.

[52] See Discussant ID 7 in Table C.1.

[53] See Discussant ID 2 in Table C.1.

[54] See Discussant ID 4 in Table C.1.

or inequity specifically tailored to what might be encountered in the course of an investigation or adjudication. Two discussants agreed that "data and training" are the highest priority areas to address.[55] Another discussant said they could see the benefit of having training for investigative staff regarding bias and pointed out that unintentional bias can shape things in interviews conducted with different communities. This discussant recommended "better training the investigative staff to work with the general public to ensure we are mitigating potential bias as best as possible" and suggested that such training "should be tailored, cover potential roadblocks, different cultures, training that is meaningful."[56] A different discussant said that with "all the training I've had, we've never talked about DEIA on an adjudication, about how we can have a bias. So I think it starts with the training modules, adding that to the training" and then went on to say, "I feel my personnel should go through DEIA training to be well equipped to do personnel vetting effectively."[57]

We did learn about nascent efforts to incorporate specific training related to cultural competence for personnel vetting staff. One discussant spoke about a new cultural sensitivity pilot training program at their organization that was built around scenarios that an investigator might encounter in the investigative process. The development of that training was triggered by a report of unacceptable treatment of an individual by an investigator as part of the security clearance investigation. The feedback received from participants after implementation of the pilot training was that it needed to be rolled out organizationwide, so now that organization is looking to build this in as required training, tailored to the job role someone is filling (e.g., investigator, adjudicator, quality reviewer).

Several discussants addressed the need for training standardization and consistent policies across agencies to institutionalize such initiatives. One discussant asserted that it is essential to

> [make] sure folks get it from the right people at the right time in the right place. The polygraphers . . . folks doing background investigations, making sure they're fully trained. I know there are some standards but a lot of standards I've seen don't include DEIA training.[58]

Another discussant said that the personnel vetting process needs a

> standardized process across all of federal government because I feel that's our weak link. If someone has 3 DUI's, for most of us that's a pattern. And ensuring one person of color isn't found unsuitable because of it and a person who is not is cleared. So taking a look at

---

[55] See Discussant ID 10 and Discussant 11 in Table C.1.

[56] See Discussant ID 7 in Table C.1.

[57] See Discussant ID 16 in Table C.1.

[58] See Discussant ID 11 in Table C.1.

that granular data to make sure we are trained to apply those extra considerations equally among all subjects.[59]

A different discussant agreed there is a need to have such training

standardized across the board so one agency isn't saying something different than other agencies. . . . It would be awesome to have the experts make an e-learning module that can be shared across the federal government, so once they get through in-person training, they go into on the job training, then . . . they're out there sitting with mentor and coach and they would see these scenarios from the system . . . and have it to refresh their memory.[60]

Related to this area of improvement, two discussants indicated that training standards are in process of being updated and will include "training standards to ensure investigators and adjudicators have cultural competence training as they go through their work in the process."[61] One discussant also informed us that there is work being done to see what related training standards might be applied to polygraph examiners, because the current training standards for investigators and adjudicators do not apply to them.

Related to standardization and policy institutionalization of recognizing potential for bias and inequity concepts, a couple discussants emphasized the need for leadership in this space, to scrutinize and improve the process to ensure that barriers are mitigated and that the potential for bias and inequity is minimized. One discussant said, "Leadership right now have championed efforts in this area" and are taking a "very active role in getting policies in place knowing these policies will live longer than any of us in these roles."[62] There were a few DEIA SMEs who acknowledged that they have encountered some resistance to cultural competence and DEIA initiatives in the workplace, and had encountered individuals who view DEIA initiatives as being political in nature. One of our discussants offered the following perspective in that vein:

I think the concepts of DEIA are somewhat controversial concepts. These are areas where intelligent people can have differences of opinion. . . . Because there are some political differences . . . half the population might take an opposing view to these ideas and we really should put limited resources to areas that have demonstrated a clear or reasonable basis to think we're doing something discriminatory. Everybody regardless of political orientation will say we're not in business of discriminating. If there's a bias we can eliminate, we'll do that. But the bar needs to be set for reasonable indication of a problem.[63]

---

[59] See Discussant ID 16 in Table C.1.

[60] See Discussant ID 6 in Table C.1.

[61] See Discussant ID 10 in Table C.1.

[62] See Discussant ID 11 in Table C.1.

[63] See Discussant ID 4 in Table C.1.

Multiple DEIA SME discussants expressed concern that some may try to weaponize what is being done in this space as far as policy and training. One discussant said it is not about advantaging or disadvantaging anyone but instead, "we would look to characterize about increasing equity within process . . . not just looking a specific demographics."[64]

Collecting and Analyzing Demographic Information

Several discussants pointed out that there are no readily available data for those who manage and assess the security clearance process to analyze whether there are bias or inequities in the process, and whether they have resulted in negative outcomes for certain populations. As one discussant explained it,

> We don't have access to data because of the way it's designed. For privacy and protection, any demographic data is often kept separate. So without data collection we can't run analysis to where exactly we may see any indication of bias.[65]

Another discussant said, "I have heard many times [from colleagues] that there is no bias—but we don't know because we are not measuring."[66] When speaking about an effort to try and assess potential inequity in one of the processes at their organization, one discussant explained,

> One thing we discovered is Security does not collect demographic info up front. That kind of handicapped us, not being able to effectively look at the [demographics] of this person going through the security process.[67]

The same discussant further expanded on this with,

> So without data collection we can't run analysis to where exactly we may see any indication of bias. Also, the security process can have multiple steps: There's the medical, polygraph, so many pieces. Without our ability to run demographic data across the board on where folks fall out and when, it's hard to figure out where the issue is to diagnose it.[68]

Many discussants supported the idea of creating a mechanism to collect relevant demographic information from job candidates so that outcomes of adjudications could be better tracked, measured, understood, and mitigated if bias or sources of inequity were apparent. One

---

[64] See Discussant ID 1 in Table C.1.

[65] See Discussant ID 10 in Table C.1.

[66] See Discussant ID 9 in Table C.1.

[67] See Discussant ID 10 in Table C.1.

[68] See Discussant ID 10 in Table C.1.

discussant said, "One key thing is to capture data—bias or not bias—capture information."[69] Another discussant said, "Say we need to do one thing, it's to say we need to start collecting demographic data from people going through the entire process."[70]

A few discussants mentioned that there was an effort under consideration by the U.S. government to include a type of survey or addendum that would be completely separate from the SF-86 and from the adjudication of the security clearance itself. Information provided by the candidate would be collected in a protected manner, and then later correlated with adjudicative outcomes for analysis. About this proposal, another discussant said,

> It would be a good pilot to know if they add that addendum if it adds more worry to the applicant. Because I know if I answer it on USA Jobs and you ask me again on background check and investigation, I would wonder why you're asking.[71]

Related to that concern, another discussant said "I think managing and tracking DEIA data through a separate process . . . and informing people about how it will be used"[72] are essential, emphasizing the importance of being transparent with candidates about what will happen with their data and establishing trust that such demographic data will be kept confidential and separate from those reviewing the case. Regarding the importance of messaging to applicants at the front end of the process, one discussant gave an example of a conversation with a prospective applicant to a national security position who told them,

> "I'm gay so I'm never going to apply" . . . so a lot of messaging has to be done up front, that's something we want to improve on to make sure people aren't making assumptions and that we're not missing out on talent before we can even get that data.[73]

Related to the lack of data available for analysis, one of our discussants pointed out that "if a study proved such biases occurred at even a fractional rate, we would prioritize training to mitigate that. But there's no indication we have a problem there."[74] Two discussants pointed out that a lack of data either way can be used by some who want to naturally defend the intended objectivity of the process as an indication that bias or inequity is not an issue rather than an indication that reliable data are not available for assessment. One discussant said that they have heard skeptical sentiments from individuals in the personnel vetting process, that "'this affects so few' and 'how do we even know it's a problem?'" and, in response, the discussant indicated they respond with "until we run that data we can't identify where

---

[69] See Discussant ID 9 in Table C.1.

[70] See Discussant ID 10 in Table C.1.

[71] See Discussant ID 13 in Table C.1.

[72] See Discussant ID 2 in Table C.1.

[73] See Discussant ID 11 in Table C.1.

[74] See Discussant ID 4 in Table C.1.

the issues are, then unfortunately you're in the limelight . . . so help me help you identify the real problem.'"[75]

Summary

Many of our discussants confirmed that the information required in the structural element of the security clearance process (shaped by the SF-86 form and the SEAD-4 guidelines) can reveal information regarding one's race or ethnicity, gender, gender identity, sexual orientation, and neurodivergence either based on assumptions or inferences that can be made as a result of the information required of an applicant. Therefore, the human element of the process, made up in part of investigators, adjudicators, and quality assurance reviewers, likely has awareness of these demographic and other factors about the individuals they are investigating and adjudicating. Human judgment and biases that apply in other employment or social contexts have the potential to manifest themselves in the human element of assessing for security clearance eligibility; several discussants provided anecdotal examples of this aspect.

Discussants offered suggestions for potential areas for improvement with regard to addressing the potential for biases and inequities in the personnel vetting process. These included addressing potentially problematic sections, questions, and language in the structural forms and guidelines that shape the personnel vetting process to address potential areas of bias and inequity. Most of our discussants supported the idea of implementing personnel vetting training related to potential for bias and inequity, requiring such training for personnel who are involved in investigating, and assessing an individual's security clearance eligibility. Finally, many discussants pointed to the need to collect and analyze demographic information to better understand whether and where bias and inequities might be occurring in the personnel vetting process.

---

[75] See Discussant ID 10 in Table C.1.

CHAPTER 4

Conclusions, Observations, and Recommendations

Detailed personal information is required from applicants as part of the background investigation process for security clearance adjudication, including information that has the potential to reveal an individual's race or ethnicity, gender, gender identity, sexual orientation, or neurodivergence. This report sought to identify elements that have the potential to contribute to bias and sources of inequity within the security clearance vetting process, which is the most detailed and comprehensive of the personnel vetting processes when it comes to investigating an individual and their past behavior.

To accomplish this goal, we reviewed previous research on employment and workplace discrimination related to race in the workplace, and also explored research on gender, gender identity, sexual orientation, and neurodivergence discrimination in employment. These reviews helped to identify potential factors that may also influence the security clearance process, which is a required part of the employment process for national security professionals. We then conducted discussions with DEIA and personnel SMEs in which we explored potential aspects of the U.S. government personnel vetting process that have the potential to contribute to bias and sources of inequity, including those related to structural and human elements of the process. These steps informed our final analysis and led us to the following conclusions, observations, and recommendations for the U.S. government to consider.

Conclusions

There is the potential for bias and sources of inequity in both the structural and human elements of the security clearance personnel vetting process. As part of a personnel vetting investigation, an individual's race or ethnicity, gender, gender identity, sexual orientation, or neurodivergence are either knowable from the documentation they are required to submit as part of the structural element of the process or can be inferred by the personnel conducting the investigative and adjudicative human elements of the process. Human judgment and biases that manifest themselves in other employment or social contexts have the potential to contribute to bias and sources of inequity in the human element of the process of determining security clearance eligibility.

Observations and Recommendations

Observation 1: Some components of the forms and guidelines that make up the structural elements of the security clearance personnel vetting process—including SF-86 (Questionnaire for National Security Positions) and Security Executive Agent Directive 4 (SEAD-4)—have the potential to contribute to bias and sources of inequity because of the nature of the information requested, the language used to request it, and the language contained in the guidelines used to adjudicate that information.

- **Recommendation 1:** Review and revise the SF-86 and SEAD-4 guidelines (and other personnel vetting forms and guidelines) to minimize the potential for bias and sources of inequity related to race or ethnicity, gender, gender identity, sexual orientation, or neurodivergence, while still collecting the information that is essential to support a national security clearance adjudicative decision. Any SF-86 revisions to this end would aim to minimize the possibility of collecting unnecessary revelatory information about individuals that has the significant potential to contribute to bias and sources of inequity in treatment and/or that could result in unintentionally deterring a diverse set of individuals from even applying to national security positions. SEAD-4 guideline review and revisions would (1) evaluate the guidelines themselves to determine whether the overall risk category of the guideline or the language contained in the guideline contribute to the potential of a biased or inequitable adjudication and (2) consider whether new or different mitigation language for the risk factor is required to minimize that potential. See Appendix A for an initial framing approach that can be used for evaluating personnel vetting forms and guidelines for potential areas that might contribute to bias or inequity.

Observation 2: Although training for some personnel vetting staff includes cognitive bias awareness, training for investigators and adjudicators does not include modules that specifically train or prepare personnel vetting staff for engagement with applicants from diverse cultures, experiences, and lifestyles.

- **Recommendation 2:** Implement standardized and tailored training to prepare individuals in the investigative and adjudicative process for interactions with applicants from diverse cultures, experiences, and lifestyles. Such tailored training would be specific the personnel vetting process, and would include investigator and adjudicator-specific curricula informed by relevant vignettes, real-world case studies, and scenarios. To ensure that there is consistent training across investigative and adjudicative service providers, existing training standards and programs for SSC personnel would need to be revised.

Observation 3: Demographic data related to racial or ethnic, gender, gender identity, sexual orientation, or neurodivergent categories are not collected or analyzed in the context of the security clearance process, limiting the ability to assess the process and adjudicative outcomes for applicants to determine whether and where bias and inequity may be occurring.

- **Recommendation 3:** Explore implementing a mechanism by which personnel vetting applicants could voluntarily and separately provide demographic information about race or ethnicity, gender, gender identity, sexual orientation, or neurodivergence (via a survey or other method) for follow-on analysis that is independent from the formal background investigation and adjudication process. Such data collection would need to include clearly articulated language that defines the purpose of the voluntary data collection; how these data would be used to review personnel vetting files and outcomes in a subsequent analysis; and how that information will be protected and who will and will not have access to it (e.g., it would not be provided to those conducting the background investigation and adjudication). A voluntary data collection effort like this would have limitations based on the number and nature of the submissions, but it could enable an initial effort to analyze whether inequities or disparities may exist in the process—beginning at the application phase, through the investigation and interviews, and ending in adjudication and appeals.

Recent Developments

The formal data collection and analysis that informed this report's conclusions, observations, and recommendations occurred between April 2022 and November 2022. In the time between the completion of our analysis and the publication of this report, several personnel vetting developments have occurred, including related to recommendations we make above. The federal government now has an effort underway to replace the standard forms and questionnaires for personnel vetting with a new proposed PVQ, which seeks to address several bias- and equity-related considerations.[1] Although the government intends to review

---

[1] On November 23, 2022, OPM submitted a 60-day notice (an Information Collection Request [ICR]) within the Federal Register to solicit public comment on proposed changes to background investigation forms. OPM's ICR seeks to create a *common form* (or PVQ) that would consolidate questions across background investigation forms (from the SF-86 and SF-85 family of forms) into a single questionnaire to streamline information-gathering. Related to DEIA, the proposed PVQ now uses gender-inclusive language; for example, the ICR explains that listing traditional binary gender categorizations would no longer be required for the PVQ, because OPM and the Office of the Director of National Intelligence concluded that asking for the respondent to indicate "male" or "female" on the form no longer has the utility in the investigative process to justify the burden of requiring that information from respondents. Traditional familial relationship status are also revised from "mother," "father," or "brother or sister" to more-inclusive and nongender specific terms that would list "parent" or "sibling." Proposed changes from the prior forms also include additional descriptions for why certain types of information (e.g., "other names used") are required, and new language intended to mitigate privacy concerns by clarifying how information that is collected will be used in the personnel vetting process. Questions related to the Selective Service record have

the SEAD-4 guidelines as part of the overall personnel vetting reform effort, we do not know at this time whether this effort will include a review that considers the potential for bias and sources of inequity. The government is also in the process of updating its training standards to include objectives and identify principles related to potential for bias and inequity for personnel vetting. These newer efforts are either under development or with implementation still in progress, so an assessment of these related and developing efforts is not included in this report's examination.

---

also been removed, and the ICR explains that such information is already collected by employing agencies through other mechanisms. The PVQ revises the psychological and emotional health questions, shifting from asking about all mental health treatment or counseling to a more tailored set of questions focused on hospitalizations and specific diagnoses. Public comment on OPM's proposed changes ended on January 23, 2023; the government is reviewing the comments received as it proceeds to roll out the PVQ to replace the SF-86 and SF-85 family of forms.

An Initial Framing Approach—Strategic Questions for Evaluating Personnel Vetting Forms and Guidelines

This appendix provides an initial framing approach that can be used for evaluating personnel vetting forms and guidelines for potential areas that might contribute to bias or inequity.[1] Although there are several sections of the SF-86 and SEAD-4 Adjudicative Guidelines, we have scoped this appendix to focus on examples using the form's Section 22 (Police Record) and Section 26 (Financial Record) relevant issues identified from our literature review in Chapter 2 and discussant observations in Chapter 3. This appendix provides a set of overarching strategic questions for consideration as a first step in developing an approach that reflects on and assesses the personnel vetting forms and guidelines that make up the structural element of the security clearance process, to help identify and mitigate the potential for bias and sources of inequity.

Example Sections

Standard Form-86 Section 22: Police Record Questions

Section 22 of the SF-86 poses a series of questions to applicants that seek to assess an individual's judgment, reliability, and trustworthiness to safeguard classified information. Such questions require applicants to list instances of arrests, court appearances, case dispositions (even if expunged), and prison time served if sentenced. Some examples of the types of questions included in Section 22 appear in Box A.1. Although some questions in this section are time-bound (within a period of seven years), others extend to the entirety of an applicant's life cycle.[2]

---

[1] We define our framing approach in line with the definition in Entman, 1993 (p. 52), which suggests that

> Frames, then, *define problems* (determine what a causal agent is doing with what costs and benefits, usually measured in terms of common cultural values); *diagnose causes*-identify the forces creating the problem ... and *suggest remedies* (offer and justify treatments for the problems and predict their likely effects.

[2] For example, the SF-86 distinguishes between time-bound sections with questions that posit "Have you EVER ..." versus, "In the last seven (7) years ..."

BOX A.1

Standard Form 86, Section 22: Police Record Questions

- In the last seven (7) years have you been issued a summons, citation, or ticket to appear in court in a criminal proceeding against you?
- In the last seven (7) years have you been arrested by any police officer, sheriff, marshal or any other type of law enforcement official?
- In the last seven (7) years have you been charged with, convicted of, or sentenced for a crime in any court?
- In the last seven (7) years have you been or are you currently on probation or parole?
- Were you sentenced as a result of this offense?
- Were you sentenced to imprisonment for a term exceeding 1 year?
- Are you currently on trial, awaiting a trial, or awaiting sentencing on criminal charges for this offense?

SOURCE: Reproduces text from OPM, 2016, p. 95.

The questionnaire provides some explanatory space for applicant answers, though is primarily limited to whether the charge occurred at a felony or misdemeanor level, the nature of the charge, and the date and outcome resulting from the charge. The questionnaire does not seek additional context from applicants for listed criminal conduct beyond simple ("yes" or "no") explanations.[3] Applicants typically are able to provide some additional mitigating information during the background interview stage, though it is possible that (1) some applicants may either self-select out of the process at this stage or (2) may not be discontinued in the personnel process if it appears they may not successfully pass adjudication at a later date.

Responses to applicant submission, investigator data collection (e.g., requesting court records), and additional clarifications provided during security processing interviews are collated and forwarded as "investigative packages" to authorized adjudicative agencies. Adjudicators then use specific sets of criteria (i.e., adjudicative guidelines) to evaluate candidates against position-based risk. A summary of SEAD-4 adjudicative guideline concerns and conditions related to Criminal Conduct (Guideline J) is in Table A.1.

We noted in Chapter 2 that criminal background checks can negatively affect application rates and callback percentages across job sectors (e.g., Bushway et al., 2020). We also noted that African Americans and Latinos are more likely than White applicants to have criminal records, an issue that could emerge during U.S. government job searches and highlighted during subsequent background investigation processes. (e.g., Alexander, 2010; Emory, 2021; Pager et al., 2009; Vuolo et al., 2017; Wakefield and Uggen, 2010). Our interviews across personnel vetting and DEIA SMEs confirmed the potential for bias related to Section 22 and Adjudicative Guideline J; one discussant noted the potential for racial bias from criminal his-

---

[3] The form includes a one-sentence space for each entry.

TABLE A.1

Adjudicative Guideline J–Criminal Conduct

Concern or Condition	Components of Guideline J
Concerns that criminal history raises	Criminal activity creates doubt about a person's judgment, reliability, and trustworthiness. By its very nature, it calls into question a person's ability or willingness to comply with laws, rules, and regulations.
Conditions that could raise security concerns	(a) a pattern of minor offenses, any one of which on its own would be unlikely to affect a national security eligibility decision, but which in combination cast doubt on the individual's judgment, reliability, or trustworthiness; (b) evidence (including, but not limited to, a credible allegation, an admission, and matters of official record) of criminal conduct, regardless of whether the individual was formally charged, prosecuted, or convicted; (c) individual is currently on parole or probation; (d) violation or revocation of parole or probation, or failure to complete a court-mandated rehabilitation program; and (e) discharge or dismissal from the Armed Forces for reasons less than "Honorable."
Conditions that could mitigate security concerns	(a) so much time has elapsed since the criminal behavior happened, or it happened under such unusual circumstances, that it is unlikely to recur and does not cast doubt on the individual's reliability, trustworthiness, or good judgment; (b) the individual was pressured or coerced into committing the act and those pressures are no longer present in the person's life; (c) no reliable evidence to support that the individual committed the offense; and (d) there is evidence of successful rehabilitation; including, but not limited to, the passage of time without recurrence of criminal activity, restitution, compliance with the terms of parole or probation, job training or higher education, good employment record, or constructive community involvement.

SOURCE: Reproduces text from CFR 32, Part 147.

tory record reporting dependent on the candidate's location, which could trigger the "over-work" issues we identified earlier in this report. Other discussants noted the potential impact of mental or developmental disabilities that may receive unfair treatment within existing criminal justice procedures.

Standard Form 86 Section 26: Financial Record Questions

Section 26 of the SF-86 poses a list of questions that inquire about a candidate's ability to "live within one's means, satisfy debts, and meet financial obligations" (Office of the Director of Intelligence, 2017). Much like with assessing an individual's criminal history, perceived issues in these areas can raise questions about an individual's reliability, trustworthiness, and ability to protect classified or sensitive information according to information contained within existing adjudicative guidelines. Box A.2 provides some examples of the questions to which applicants respond. Because the form is used primarily as a screening mechanism,

BOX A.2

Sample Questions from SF-86 Section 26: Financial Record Questions

- Have you EVER experienced financial problems due to gambling?
- In the last seven (7) years have you failed to file or pay Federal, state, or other taxes when required by law or ordinance? Did you fail to file, pay as required, or both?
- In the last seven (7) years have you been counseled, warned, or disciplined for violating the terms of agreement for a travel or credit card provided by your employer?
- Are you currently utilizing, or seeking assistance from, a credit counseling service or other similar resource to resolve your financial difficulties?
- In the last seven (7) years, you have been delinquent on alimony or child support payments.
- In the last seven (7) years, you had a judgment entered against you.
- In the last seven (7) years, you had a lien placed against your property for failing to pay taxes or other debts.
- You are currently delinquent on any Federal debt.
- In the last seven (7) years, you had any possessions or property voluntarily or involuntarily repossessed or foreclosed?
- In the last seven (7) years, you defaulted on any type of loan?
- In the last seven (7) years, you had bills or debts turned over to a collection agency?
- In the last seven (7) years, you had any account or credit card suspended, charged off, or cancelled for failing to pay as agreed?
- In the last seven (7) years, you were evicted for non-payment?
- In the last seven (7) years, you had wages, benefits, or assets garnished or attached for any reason?

SOURCE: Reproduces text from OPM, 2016, pp. 115-121.

spaces provided for explanation beyond short descriptions of an event may not capture larger DEIA components.

Applicant-provided information, financial record data retrieval (e.g., Fair Credit Reporting Disclosure and Authorization information received via Fair Credit Reporting Act, codified at 15 U.S.C. § 1681 et seq.), and additional information gained through security interviews are also provided via investigative packages to adjudicators. Adjudicators use adjudicative guidelines to evaluate candidates against conditions that could both raise and mitigate a list of security concerns. A summary of SEAD-4 adjudicative guideline concerns and conditions related to Guideline F–Financial Considerations are in Table A.2.

Our literature review in Chapter 2 highlighted that racial wage gaps have occurred irrespective of education level or skill level across labor markets (e.g., Wilson and Darity, 2022). We also noted that the literature on bias within labor markets finds that racial stratification will continue to contribute toward racial wage gaps and inhibit social mobility and, therefore, could

TABLE A.2

Adjudicative Guideline F–Financial Considerations

Concern or Condition	Component of Guideline F
Concerns that financial problems raise	Failure to live within one's means, satisfy debts, and meet financial obligations may indicate poor self-control, lack of judgment, or unwillingness to abide by rules and regulations, all of which can raise questions about an individual's reliability, trustworthiness, and ability to protect classified or sensitive information. Financial distress can also be caused or exacerbated by, and thus can be a possible indicator of, other issues of personnel security concern such as excessive gambling, mental health conditions, substance misuse, or alcohol abuse or dependence. An individual who is financially overextended is at greater risk of having to engage in illegal or otherwise questionable acts to generate funds. Affluence that cannot be explained by known sources of income is also a security concern insofar as it may result from criminal activity, including espionage.
Conditions that could raise security concerns	(a) inability to satisfy debts; (b) unwillingness to satisfy debts regardless of the ability to do so; (c) a history of not meeting financial obligations; (d) deceptive or illegal financial practices such as embezzlement, employee theft, check fraud, expense account fraud, mortgage fraud, filing deceptive loan statements and other intentional financial breaches of trust; (e) consistent spending beyond one's means or frivolous or irresponsible spending, which may be indicated by excessive indebtedness, significant negative cash flow, a history of late payments or of non-payment, or other negative financial indicators; (f) failure to file or fraudulently filing annual Federal, state, or local income tax returns or failure to pay annual Federal, state, or local income tax as required; (g) unexplained affluence, as shown by a lifestyle or standard of living, increase in net worth, or money transfers that are inconsistent with known legal sources of income; (h) borrowing money or engaging in significant financial transactions to fund gambling or pay gambling debts; and (i) concealing gambling losses, family conflict, or other problems caused by gambling.

Table A.2—Continued

Concern or Condition	Component of Guideline F
Conditions that could mitigate security concerns	(a) the behavior happened so long ago, was so infrequent, or occurred under such circumstances that it is unlikely to recur and does not cast doubt on the individual's current reliability, trustworthiness, or good judgment; (b) the conditions that resulted in the financial problem were largely beyond the person's control (e.g., loss of employment, a business downturn, unexpected medical emergency, a death, divorce or separation, clear victimization by predatory lending practices, or identity theft), and the individual acted responsibly under the circumstances; (c) the individual has received or is receiving financial counseling for the problem from a legitimate and credible source, such as a non-profit credit counseling service, and there are clear indications that the problem is being resolved or is under control; (d) the individual initiated and is adhering to a good-faith effort to repay overdue creditors or otherwise resolve debts; (e) the individual has a reasonable basis to dispute the legitimacy of the past-due debt which is the cause of the problem and provides documented proof to substantiate the basis of the dispute or provides evidence of actions to resolve the issue; (f) the affluence resulted from a legal source of income; and (g) the individual has made arrangements with the appropriate tax authority to file or pay the amount owed and is in compliance with those arrangements.

SOURCE: Reproduces text from CFR 32, Part 147, pp. 15–16.

affect required applicant responses (and U.S. government subjective judgments) if not mitigated through form revision and awareness training (Recommendations 1 and 3 in Chapter 4).[4]

An Initial Framing Approach with Strategic Questions

The application of this framing approach to examine personnel vetting forms and guidelines is intended to help to identify areas for potential revision to minimize and mitigate the effects of potential bias and other obstacles related to DEIA that may inhibit access to national security positions. The initial framing approach in this section is derived in part based on our literature review and our discussions with personnel vetting and DEIA SMEs, and also informed by separate literature on enabling organizational learning through reflexive inquiry.[5] This

---

[4] For example, we cited the Ballance, Clifford, and Shoag (2020) finding that, even in areas where employers are prevented from using credit checks as part of the hiring and screening process, employers may still engage in statistical discrimination.

[5] For example, some questions draw from the use of reflexive questioning, a method of generating learning opportunities to (re)examine organizational structures, values, beliefs, or judgments. Reflexive-based questions are used in a variety of settings to generate insight, including academia, family or group therapy, health care settings, and conflict resolution. See, for example, Winslade and Monk, 2000; Winslade, 2009; and Bruner, 1990.

initial framing approach is intended to assist personnel vetting stakeholders to critically re-examine assumptions contained within investigation forms and adjudicative guidelines.

Strategic Questions

The following strategic questions are intended to serve as a guide as SSC policymakers and stakeholder consider re-evaluating of the questions embedded within background investigation forms and associated adjudicative guidelines (see Table A.3). These questions are designed to facilitate discussions about equity in personnel vetting policies, processes, and procedures. The questions presented in this appendix primarily focus on existing investigation forms—although they could be expanded to examine related documents (e.g., "why is the question being asked" versus "why are we developing this policy") and to potentially inform future investigator and adjudicator training in line with revisions to forms and guidelines over time. The key objective of these questions is to introduce reflection upon long-standing assumptions embedded within the investigative and adjudicative process. That is, these questions may be used as a framework to challenge the assumptions, logic, and evaluative statements embedded throughout the investigation and adjudication process, ultimately with the goal of fostering a critical look at the forms and guidance, and to also encourage organizational learning.

TABLE A.3

Summary Framing Approach for Strategic Questions to Identify Potential Biases and Sources of Inequity in Personnel Vetting Forms and Guidelines

Strategic Question	Purpose
Why is this question being asked, and/or why is this information being collected?	To deconstruct questions and add nuance to binary ("yes" or "no") security questions
Why do we have to ask this question and/or collect this information?	To (re)examine requirements or other authorities
Does this question and/or information request acknowledge potential unequal access to resources?	To generate greater understanding of external (societal) bias and impacts on marginalized populations and to generate/ understand barriers to entry via empathy (applicant point of view)
Does this phrasing of this question or the adjudicative guideline behind it conflict with or reflect emerging societal norms?	To construct inclusive questions that still collect the required information but also ensure questions and guidelines maintain pace with evolving policy, norms, and regulations, as appropriate.
Does this question and/or collection of the information enable or inhibit a more diverse workforce?	To help connect logic of investigation forms and guidelines to evolving U.S. government DEIA initiatives

SOURCE: Features information from authors' analysis of literature related to structural biases.

Strategic Question 1: Why is this question being asked, and/or why is this information being collected? This is a deceptively complex question. The purpose of this question is to deconstruct the logical premise or basis for why the question appears on the form, including deconstructing questions beyond traditional binary ("yes" or "no") answers. Using this simple question begins to move the inquiry away from "we are asking this question to determine eligibility to classified information" to "why are we asking this particular question to determine eligibility to classified information?" This initial strategic question could set conditions for subsequent organizational learning (Sluzki, 1992; White, 2007).[6] For example, a question focused on criminal history information may gain valuable information about an individual's past behavior in terms of identified risk factors, but how it is phrased could also potentially filter out applicants, perhaps before they complete the questionnaire, who may or may not actually meet institutional definitions of trustworthiness. Furthermore, such security questions may presume that having been arrested for a crime in the past is correlated with a propensity to break the law in the future, which again, may or may not be true in the context of other factors. Therefore, some security questions, as written, may have embedded value statements (various levels of subjectivity) as applicants interpret whether and how best to respond and investigators/adjudicators evaluate their responses. The intent here is to take a critical eye to security questions to assess why they are being asked in the context of the requirement to assess risk and make a trust judgment.

Strategic Question 2: Why do we have to ask this question and/or collect this information? This question is closely related to the first question, although it seeks to understand the foundations (structural logic) for the question as part of an investigative form or in support of an adjudicative guideline—for example, asking, "What requirement mandates inclusion of criminal history on security forms? Is this question necessary and relevant to accurately assess risk to national security (and, if so, why)?" This second strategic question may be used to help uncover or re-examine outdated sections that do not aid investigations—or that may require revision to increase applicant accessibility (e.g., confusing or poorly worded prompts). If the question is connected to a requirement, that requirement might also be assessed taking into account any DEIA-related implications. For example, questions as phrased that are focused on Psychological and Emotional Health (Section 21) have the potential to have applicants select out of screening processes based on their mental health history or experiences and may not fully acknowledge disparities in high-quality mental health treatment that may mitigate risk presented by certain diagnoses. Similarly, questions about drug use may not currently account for larger/societal challenges and socioeconomic differences focused on chemical dependency within the U.S. pandemic (e.g., fentanyl), associated costs of addiction-treatment centers, or other inabilities to travel long-distances to outpatient clinics.

Strategic Question 3: Does this question and/or information request acknowledge potential unequal access to resources? This question could be used on its own or in tandem

---

[6] This approach is known as *scaffolding* within the academic literature. See, for example, White, 2007; and Sluzki, 1992.

with other strategic questions listed in this section to identify the potential for bias across SF-86 categories (and adjudicative guidelines). For example, SF-86 questions pertaining to criminal, financial, substance abuse, or mental health issues are generally binary ("in the last 7 years, have you . . . or have you EVER . . .") which may (or may not if rejected from the process) be further explored in an applicant interview. However, such questions do not explicitly provide considerations of the types of accesses and resources available to minority or marginalized communities. For example, a candidate who is able to secure expert legal representation may not ever enter the criminal justice system (i.e., generate a CHRI record), whereas another candidate may have no choice but to rely on an assigned public defender. Similarly, a candidate who loses a job, potentially through a form of employment discrimination, may accrue more debt than a candidate who has not faced barriers related to discrimination and may have access to a higher-paying job.

Strategic Question 4: Does the phrasing of this question and/or collection of the information conflict with or reflect emerging societal norms? Multiple discussants (Chapter 3) noted that U.S. government policy is often outpaced by societal changes. For example, some personnel vetting adjudicative guidelines in the past pointed to homosexual behavior as problematic, in part, because of the risk of blackmail (Director of Central Intelligence Directive No. 1/14 and Annex A Adjudication Guidelines, 1976). Concerns expressed by several of our discussants suggest that some aspects of the forms have not kept pace with LGBTQ+ considerations, rendering some questions outdated and/or potentially deterring candidates from proceeding with the national security screening process.

Strategic Question 5: Does this question and/or collection of the information enable or inhibit a more diverse workforce? Question 5 may either be deployed on its own at the end of the re-examination (or form/guideline validation) process, or in tandem with the other strategic questions. Using relevant EOs and other DEIA policy and guidance can help practitioners ensure that the personnel vetting process is consistent with evolving U.S. government policy requirements to ensure a trusted and a diverse workforce.[7]

Tables A.4 and A.5 provide worked examples focused on the criminal conduct and financial considerations adjudicative guidelines, respectively, to apply the strategic framing questions we suggest in Table A.5. The worked examples are not intended to depict a comprehensive list of questions or categories that could develop organically during the evaluation process.

---

[7] EO 14035 (2021) offers several factors that could be used to examine existing security questions. For example, does the question consider the

> (1) "many communities, identities, races, ethnicities, backgrounds, abilities, cultures, and beliefs of the American people, including underserved communities," (*Diversity*); 2) "the consistent and systematic fair, just, and impartial treatment of all individuals, including individuals who belong to underserved communities that have been denied such treatment?" (*Equity*); 3) "recognition and appreciation of employees of all backgrounds" (*Inclusion*); and 4) "providing access in a format, and on a platform that allows for people with a physical or attitudinal disability to provide adequate information" (*Accessibility*).

TABLE A.4

A Worked Example Using Strategic Framing Questions—Criminal Conduct

SF-86 Question

In the last seven (7) years have you been charged with, convicted of, or sentenced for a crime in any court?

SEAD-4 Adjudicative Guideline J Concern–Criminal Conduct

Criminal activity creates doubt about a person's judgment, reliability, and trustworthiness. By its very nature, it calls into question a person's ability or willingness to comply with laws, rules, and regulations.

Question	Consideration
Why is this question being asked, and/or why is this information being collected?	Consideration: What is the correlation (evidentiary basis) between criminal activity and judgement, reliability, and trustworthiness?
Why do we have to ask this question and/or collect this information?	Consideration: What policy requirement mandates that we ask this question? Is that requirement based on human experience? Is there empirical evidence that relates criminal history recency (7 years) with an individual's willingness to comply with future laws?
Does this question and/or information request acknowledge potential unequal access to resources?	Consideration: Does applicant access (or lack of access) to adequate legal resources in addressing the potential criminal conduct factor in to how the fact of the conduct is adjudicated? Should it be a factor?
Does this phrasing of this question or the adjudicative guideline behind it conflict with or reflect emerging societal norms?	Consideration: Related to both the substance abuse and criminal conduct adjudicative guidelines, do the forms and guidelines account for recent substance legalization/changes across various U.S. states? Should they, and what should be changed?
Does this question and/or collection of the information enable or inhibit a more diverse workforce?	Consideration: Does the question or phrasing of the guideline potentially exclude or deter specific populations, or cause skilled applicants to self "select out" of the vetting process?

Summary

The initial framing approach explored in this appendix offers several strategic questions for consideration as a potential first step in assessing how personnel vetting forms and guidelines might be evaluated for potential bias or inequity. We used SSF-86's Section 22 (Police Record) and Section 26 (Financial Record) as examples and considered how these strategic questions could be applied to reflect on the questions in those sections (and parallel SEAD-4 guidelines), related to potential bias or discrimination issues identified in our literature review in Chapter 2, discussant observations in Chapter 3, and additional literature on organizational learning through reflexive inquiry. The intent of this initial framing approach is to provide a place to start to critically re-examine assumptions and evaluate the forms and guidelines that make up the structural element of the security clearance process, with the intent to identify and mitigate the potential for bias and sources of inequity.

TABLE A.5

A Worked Example Using Strategic Framing Questions—Financial Considerations

SF-86 Question
In the last seven (7) years, you had bills or debts turned over to a collection agency?

SEAD-4 Adjudicative Guideline F Concern–Financial Considerations
Failure to live within one's means, satisfy debts, and meet financial obligations may indicate poor self-control, lack of judgment, or unwillingness to abide by rules and regulations, all of which can raise questions about an individual's reliability, trustworthiness, and ability to protect classified or sensitive information. Financial distress can also be caused or exacerbated by, and thus can be a possible indicator of, other issues of personnel security concern such as excessive gambling, mental health conditions, substance misuse, or alcohol abuse or dependence. An individual who is financially overextended is at a greater risk of having to engage in illegal or otherwise questionable acts to generate funds. Affluence that cannot be explained by known sources of income is also a security concern insofar as it may result from criminal activity, including espionage.

Question	Consideration
Why is this question being asked, and/or why is this information being collected?	Consideration: What evidence supports the linkage between having bills or debts turned over to a collection agency and a lack of judgement and/or unwillingness to abide by rules and regulations?
Why do we have to ask this question and/or collect this information?	Consideration: What policy requirement or regulation mandates that we ask this question? Has the statement that financial distress is indicative of gambling, mental health conditions, or other substance abuse issues born out in other adjudications?
Does this question and/or information request acknowledge potential unequal access to resources?	Consideration: Is unemployment, or other economic disparities related to minority or marginalized communities factored into the adjudicative approach? Should it be?
Does the phrasing of this question or the adjudicative guideline behind it conflict with or reflect emerging societal norms?	Consideration: Are emerging circumstances that may affect minority or marginalized communities disproportionately being considered in the process (e.g., financial distress and potential debt delinquency/unemployment due to pandemic related job loss, lack of resources and/or ability to work remotely)? Should they be?
Does this question and/or collection of the information enable or inhibit a more diverse workforce?	Consideration: Could the question or adjudicative concern, as phrased, discourage (exclude) potential applicants who may have experienced some of those described issues (e.g., mental health conditions which are unspecified in the guideline) from applying to federal employment?

APPENDIX B

Literature Review Methods

We reviewed literature on race, gender, gender identity, sexual orientation, and neurodivergence and how it relates to workplace inequality. Because racial inequality was the initial the primary focus of this study, we conducted a comprehensive review of race and ethnicity related to workplace inequality. We added an additional narrative review of literature on gender, gender identity, sexual orientation, and neurodivergence and how they relate to workplace inequality.

Literature Review on Racial Inequality and Workplace Discrimination

We conducted a comprehensive literature review of research on racial differences in employment outcomes. The review took place in two phases. First, we conducted a keyword search of relevant research from 2002 to 2022. Table B.1 provides a list of keywords used and databases searched. In total, the search yielded 659 sources.

Second, once the search was complete, we conducted a three-level review of the sources using DistillerSR literature review software.

TABLE B.1
Literature Review Keyword Search

Selected Keywords[a]	Databases
Employment, Discrimination, Job applicant screening, Race, African American, Person of color, Latino, Asian, Native American	Scopus, Business Source Complete, APA PsychInfo, Web of Science and Sociological Abstracts, Criminal Justice Abstracts, Index to Legal Periodicals and Books

[a] Keywords listed served as a base for the search and permutations were used to increase search results.

TABLE B.2
Literature Review Source Types

Peer-Reviewed Journal Articles	Books	Policy Report/Brief	Conference Papers/ Proceedings	Dissertations	Op-Ed/ Commentaries	Other
373	2	1	1	1	1	3

Level 1

For Level 1 of the DistillerSR review, we reviewed the title and abstract of each source and excluded sources that were not focused on (1) workplace inequality, (2) race, and/or (3) the United States. A total of 382 sources were included for subsequent review and 278 were excluded because they were determined not to be relevant to the study. Table C.2 provides a description of the types of sources reviewed.

Level 2

For Level 2 of the DistillerSR review, we conducted a second title and abstract review to exclude any sources that were not focused on the hiring process because of our study's focus specifically on the potential for bias during the hiring phase. In total, 295 sources were categorized as focusing on hiring process discrimination and 122 were categorized as focusing on post-hiring process discrimination (with some overlap between the categories).

Level 3

For Level 3 of the DistillerSR review, we conducted a full-text review of the 295 sources focused on hiring process discrimination. We answered the following series of questions in DistillerSR about the sources:

- What is the source's research question(s)
- What type of data were used in the analysis?
- When were the data collected?
- What were the main findings?
- Do the findings focus on?
  - racial bias
  - gender bias
  - the implications for the SF-86?

Once the Level 3 review was completed, results were used to identify main themes for discussion in the final report.

Literature Review on Gender, LGBTQ+ Identity, Neurodiversity, and Workplace Discrimination

Although the initial and primary focus of the descriptive literature review was the potential for racial bias, we also conducted a narrative review of literature on gender bias, LGBTQ+ bias, and neurodiversity bias in employment, based in part on sponsor interest in us further exploring these topics. For these topics, informal keyword searches were conducted to identify relevant literature and limited full-text reviews of identified sources were reviewed.

Discussant List and Discussion Protocols

This appendix provides an anonymized summary list of our discussants with U.S. government vetting and DEIA SMEs and external SMEs (see Table C.1). We also present the semi-structured protocols that were used as guides during our informal discussions with these SMEs.

TABLE C.1

Discussant ID List

Identifier	Summarized Information on Discussants
Discussant ID 1	DEIA program manager at U.S. government department/agency
Discussant ID 2	DEIA program manager at U.S. government department/agency
Discussant ID 3	DEIA program manager at U.S. government department/agency
Discussant ID 4	U.S. government personnel vetting SME with adjudicative and investigative experience
Discussant ID 6	U.S. government SME focused on training and education
Discussant ID 7	U.S. government personnel vetting SME with investigative and field experience
Discussant ID 8	U.S. government personnel vetting SME with adjudicative and quality review experience
Discussant ID 9	Former U.S. government personnel vetting SME
Discussant ID 10	DEIA program manager at U.S. government department/agency
Discussant ID 11	U.S. government personnel vetting SME
Discussant ID 12	U.S. government personnel vetting SME
Discussant ID 13	DEIA program manager at U.S. government department/agency
Discussant ID 15	DEIA SME in the private sector with former government experience
Discussant ID 16	U.S. government personnel vetting SME
Discussant ID 17	DEIA SME in the private sector
Discussant ID 19	DEIA program manager at U.S. government department/agency
Discussant ID 21	U.S. government personnel vetting SME with investigative experience
Discussant ID 22	U.S. government SME focused on training and education
Discussant ID 25	U.S. government personnel vetting SME with adjudicative experience
Discussant ID 26	U.S. government personnel vetting SME with investigative experience

Recruitment and Consent: U.S. Government Personnel Vetting and DEIA Expert Discussions

How Bias Might Manifest Itself in the Personnel Vetting Process

The Performance Accountability Council (PAC) Program Management Office (PMO) has contracted with the National Defense Research Institute—a federally funded research and development center at the RAND Corporation—to conduct a study to (1) identify key theories and practices within the social sciences literature to analyze personnel vetting processes for the potential for racial or other bias, (2) consider elements of the U.S. government personnel vetting process (e.g., questions, adjudicative guidelines, personnel) that may contribute to bias, and potentially exclude skilled candidates, and (3) develop recommendations to address vetting areas that may warrant diversity, equity, inclusion, and accessibility (DEIA) improvements.

The purpose of our discussion with you today is to learn more about (1) elements in the personnel vetting process that have the potential to contribute to racial or other bias, (2) any ongoing DEIA initiatives or training, in particular those related to the vetting process, and (3) any other information that you feel may be helpful to this research. Participation in these interviews is voluntary. Individuals can choose not to participate, to skip any questions they would rather not discuss, or to stop the interview at any time.

During the interview our project team will take notes to ensure we have an accurate record of our discussion. The notes are confidential, which means only the project team will have access to them, and there are safeguards in place to protect them. After the study is complete, all information that could identify any interviewees will be destroyed.

At the end of our study, the project team will share analysis of the interviews in a report for the PAC PMO. Our intent is to identify themes and observations from across our interviews rather than focus on one organization's perspective. The project team will take care not to provide details that could identify interviewees personally, although it may report findings by type of organization, such as private sector or other Federal agency, or by general role of individuals in the initiative (e.g., policy development, implementation, assessment).

We expect the discussion will take no more than 60 minutes. We will be holding this discussion at the UNCLASSIFIED level, but if we need to arrange for a separate classified component to the discussion, please let us know and we can make arrangements.

We appreciate and value your participation. If you are willing to participate in this study, we will get started with the discussion now.

If you have any questions about this study, please contact the project leaders:
Sina Beaghley
(310) 393-0411 x6653
beaghley@rand.org
Jessica Paige
(703) 413-1100 x5885
jpaige@rand.org

If you have questions about your rights as a research participant or need to report a research-related injury or concern, you can contact RAND's Human Subjects Protection Committee toll-free at (866) 697-5620 or by emailing hspcinfo@rand.org. If possible, when you contact the Committee, please reference Study #2022-N0105. Thank you!

Semistructured Protocol for U.S. Government Personnel Vetting Expert Discussions

1. **Can you tell us about your professional background, your current role in your organization, and your primary responsibilities?**
   a. Has your organization designated any specific roles or personnel to champion Trusted Workforce initiatives or implementation?
   b. Is there a department/office maintains DEIA responsibilities during the hiring and personnel vetting processes (e.g., HR)? Are there any DEIA-related policies/ initiatives you are aware of, in particular related to personnel vetting?
   c. Has your organization developed guidance/policy related to personnel vetting and DEIA?

2. **Are there any areas within the existing personnel vetting process that you feel may benefit from an increased examination related to DEIA policies or practices?**
   a. Are there aspects of the process that you think may be prone to potential racial, gender identification/sexual orientation, or neurodiversity bias?
   b. Are there any instances where you witnessed or were made aware of potential bias?
   a. Are there any sections or questions within the SF-86/85/85p (security clearance/ suitability questionnaire) that you feel have the potential to have adverse impacts on particular populations? [*SF-86 section list as prompt*]
   a. In your experience, do any of the existing security clearance adjudication guidelines—or the application of them—present potential areas where bias could be introduced? [*Adjudicative guidelines list as prompt*]

3. **Are you aware of any types of DEIA training available to investigative service providers, adjudicators, quality reviewer personnel, etc.?**
   a. If so, what is the nature/what are the objectives of the training? Is the training focused on personnel vetting, specifically, or more general in nature?
   b. Are you aware of any specific barriers encountered to receiving (or administering) DEIA training (e.g. funding, organizational priorities)?
   c. How are any DEIA-related training materials administered, and/or what is the frequency?

    d. To your knowledge, has there been any attempt to analyze the diversity of the investigators, adjudicators, and others with influence in the personnel vetting process?

4. If any, what recommendations might you have to improve any aspect of the personnel vetting process with regard to addressing potential for bias or DEIA considerations?

5. Is there anyone else in this space or who may have a valuable perspective who you think we should speak with?

6. Is there anything else you want to add or think we should know but haven't asked?

Semistructured Protocol for DEIA Expert Discussions

1. **Can you tell us about your professional background, your current role in your organization, and your primary responsibilities?**

    a. Has your organization designated any specific roles to champion USG-wide DEIA initiatives? If not, what position/office may have taken on DEIA initiatives?

    b. Which office maintains DEIA responsibilities during the hiring and personnel vetting processes? (e.g., HR, Employee Resource Groups, or Affinity Groups)

    c. What guidance or polices (or external resources/research) do you use/reference when crafting or implementing DEIA initiatives? Has your organization developed guidance/policy related to personnel vetting and DEIA?

    d. To your knowledge, have any recent DEIA initiatives/developments led to any personnel vetting process reviews or consideration of policy/guidance revisions?

2. **Are there any areas within the existing personnel vetting process that you feel may benefit from an increased examination related to DEIA policies or practices?**

    a. Are there aspects of the process that you think may be prone to potential racial, gender identification/sexual orientation, or neurodiversity bias?

    b. Are there any instances where you witnessed or were made aware of potential bias?

    c. To the degree that you are familiar, are there any sections or questions within the SF-86/85/85p (security clearance/suitability questionnaire) that you feel have the potential to have adverse impacts on particular populations? *[SF-86 section list as prompt]*

    d. To the degree that you are familiar, do any of the existing security clearance adjudication guidelines—or the application of them—present potential areas where bias could be introduced? *[Adjudicative guidelines list as prompt]*

3. **Are you aware of any types of DEIA training available to investigative service providers, adjudicators, quality reviewer personnel, etc.?**

    a. If so, what is the nature/what are the objectives of the training? Is the training focused on personnel vetting, specifically, or more general in nature?

    b.   Are you aware of any specific barriers encountered to receiving (or administering) DEIA training (e.g. funding, organizational priorities)?

    c.   How are any DEIA-related training materials administered, and/or what is the frequency?

    d.   To your knowledge, has there been any effort to analyze the diversity of the investigators, adjudicators, and others with influence in the personnel vetting process?

4.   If any, what recommendations might you have to improve any aspect of the personnel vetting process with regard to addressing potential for bias or DEIA considerations?

5.   Is there anyone else in this space or who may have a valuable perspective who you think we should speak with?

6.   Is there anything else you want to add or think we should know but haven't asked?

Dedoose Discussion Analysis Coding Scheme

Once the semistructured discussions were completed, we conducted both a manual thematic analysis of the notes by multiple team members and a systematic coding of the notes using Dedoose qualitative data analysis software. Here we describe the coding scheme developed for the Dedoose analysis. Codes were developed deductively and inductively, drawing from the study's research questions and main themes discussed during interviews. Table D.1 provides an overview of codes used.

TABLE D.1
Summary of Codes Used in Dedoose Qualitative Data Analysis

Coding Family	Selected Codes
Perceptions of hiring phase	Racial bias in hiring phase • Racial bias exists • Racial bias does not exist • Respondent has not noticed racial bias Gender bias in hiring phase • Gender bias exists • Gender bias does not exist • Respondent has not noticed gender bias SOGI bias • SOGI bias exists • SOGI bias does not exist • Respondent has not noticed gender bias Neurodiversity bias • Neurodiversity bias exists • Neurodiversity bias does not exist • Respondent has not noticed neurodiversity bias

Table D.1—Continued

Coding Family	Selected Codes
Perceptions of background investigation phase	Racial bias in background investigation • Racial bias exists • Racial bias does not exist • Respondent has not noticed racial bias Gender bias in background investigation phase • Gender bias exists • Gender bias does not exist • Respondent has not noticed gender bias SOGI bias in background investigation phase • SOGI bias exists • SOGI bias does not exist • Respondent has not noticed SOGI bias Neurodiversity in background investigation phase • Neurodiversity bias exists • Neurodiversity bias does not exist • Respondent has not noticed neurodiversity bias
SF-86	Potential problems with questions • Racial bias • Gender bias • SOGI bias • Neurodiversity bias • No potential problems with questions
Perceptions of adjudication phase	Racial bias in adjudication phase • Racial bias exists • Racial bias does not exist • Respondent has not noticed racial bias Gender bias in adjudication phase • Gender bias exists • Gender bias does not exist • Respondent has not noticed gender bias SOGI bias in adjudication phase • SOGI bias exists • SOGI bias does not exist • Respondent has not noticed SOGI bias Neurodiversity bias in adjudication phase • Neurodiversity bias exists • Neurodiversity bias does not exist • Respondent has not noticed neurodiversity bias
Adjudicative guidelines	Potential problems with guidelines • Racial bias • Gender bias • SOGI bias • Neurodiversity bias Respondent noted no problems with guidelines
Training	DEI training needed • For investigators • For adjudicators DEI training not needed • Respondent engaged in DEI work

Table D.1—Continued

Coding Family	Selected Codes
Recommendations to reduce potential bias	• Diversify investigator staff • Diversify adjudicator staff • Diversify general workforce
Perceptions of support for DEIA efforts	Organizational support for DEIA efforts • Supportive • Mixed support • No support • Leadership support for DEIA efforts • Supportive • Mixed support • No support

NOTE: SOGI = sexual orientation and gender identity.

Abbreviations

ADHD	attention-deficit/hyperactivity disorder
CFR	Code of Federal Regulations
CHRI	criminal history record information
DCSA	Defense Counterintelligence Security Agency
DEIA	diversity, equity, inclusion and accessibility
EARN	Employer Assistance and Resource Network on Disability Inclusion
EO	Executive Order
EOD	entry on duty
FFRDC	federally funded research and development center
GAO	U.S. Government Accountability Office
HBCU	historically Black colleges and universities
ICR	information collection request
ISP	investigative service provider
IT	information technology
LGBTQ+	lesbian, gay, bisexual, transgender, queer or questioning, and other identities
ML	machine learning
NDRI	National Defense Research Institute
NFW	Neurodiverse Federal Workforce
NGA	National Geospatial-Intelligence Agency
NSM-3	National Security Memorandum on Revitalizing America's Foreign Policy and National Security Workforce, Institutions, and Partnerships
NSRD	National Security Research Division
OCRC	Ohio Civil Rights Commission
OPM	U.S. Office of Personnel Management
PAC PMO	Performance Accountability Council Program Management Office
PVQ	Personnel Vetting Questionnaire
PWI	predominantly White institution
SEAD-4	Security Executive Agent Directive 4
SF	Standard Form
SME	subject-matter expert

| SSC | Security, Suitability, and Credentialing |
| TW | Trusted Workforce |

References

1 Half and Ten and The Sentencing Project, "Poverty and Opportunity Profile: Americans with Criminal Records," August 2022.

Alexander, Michelle, *The New Jim Crow: Mass Incarceration in the Age of Colorblindness*, New Press, 2010.

American Psychological Association, *Dictionary of Psychology*, 2023.

Annie E. Casey Foundation, *Race Equity and Inclusion Action Guide*, January 8, 2015.

Ballance, Joshua, Robert Clifford, and Daniel Shoag, "No More Credit Score: Employer Credit Check Bans and Signal Substitution," *Labour Economics*, Vol. 63, April 1, 2020.

Bendick, Marc, Rekha Rodriguez, and Sarumathi Jayaraman, "Employment Discrimination in Upscale Restaurants: Evidence from Matched Pair Testing," *Fuel and Energy Abstracts*, Vol. 47, December 2010.

Bergen, Nicole, and Ronald Labonté, "'Everything Is Perfect, and We Have No Problems': Detecting and Limiting Social Desirability Bias in Qualitative Research," *Qualitative Health Research*, Vol. 30, No. 5, 2020.

Bertrand, Marianne, and Sendhil Mullainathan, "Are Emily and Greg More Employable than Lakisha and Jamal? A Field Experiment on Labor Market Discrimination," *American Economic Review*, Vol. 94, No. 4, 2004.

Brame, Robert, Shawn D. Bushway, Ray Paternoster, and Michael G. Turner, "Demographic Patterns of Cumulative Arrest Prevalence by Ages 18 and 23," *Crime & Delinquency*, Vol. 60, No. 3, April 2014.

Bruner, Jerome, *Acts of Meaning*, Harvard University Press, 1990.

Bushway, Shawn, Irineo Cabreros, Jessica Welburn Paige, Daniel Schwam, and Jeffrey B. Wenger, "Barred from Employment: More than Half of Unemployed Men in Their 30s Had a Criminal History of Arrest," *Science Advances*, Vol. 8, No. 7, February 2022.

Caminiti, Susan, "JP Morgan Chase, Microsoft Among Growing Number of Companies Turning to Neurodiverse Workers to Help Meet Need for Talent," CNBC, April 20, 2022.

Cerda-Jara, Michael, Aminah Elster, and David J. Harding, "Criminal Record Stigma in the College-Educated Labor Market," Institute for Research on Labor and Employment, May 2020.

Code of Federal Regulations, Title 32, National Defense.

Code of Federal Regulations, Title 32, National Defense; Subtitle A, Department of Defense; Chapter I, Office of the Secretary of Defense; Subchapter D, Personnel, Military and Civilian; Part 147, Adjudicative Guidelines for Determining Eligibility for Access to Classified Information.

Code of Federal Regulations, Title 32, National Defense; Subtitle B, Other Regulations Relating to National Security; Chapter XX, Information Security Oversight Office, National Archives, and records Administration; Part 2001, Classified National Security Information.

Crenshaw, Kimberlé, "Demarginalizing the Intersection of Race and Sex: A Black Feminist Critique of Antidiscrimination Doctrine, Feminist Theory and Antiracist Politics," in Katherine Bartlett, ed., *Feminist Legal Theory: Readings in Law and Gender*, Routledge, 2013.

Davis, Tre, "Airman Advocates for Neurodiversity in Military," Air Force News Service, August 6, 2021.

DCSA—*See* Defense Counterintelligence and Security Agency.

Dedoose, homepage, undated. As of July 12, 2023:
https://www.dedoose.com

Defense Counterintelligence and Security Agency, "About Us," webpage, undated-a. As of July 7, 2023:
https://www.dcsa.mil/about/

Defense Counterintelligence and Security Agency, "Continuous Vetting," webpage, undated-b. As of July 7, 2023:
https://www.dcsa.mil/mc/pv/cv/

Defense Counterintelligence and Security Agency, "Personnel Security," webpage, undated-c. As of July 7, 2023:
https://www.dcsa.mil/Personnel-Security/

Defense Counterintelligence and Security Agency, "Investigations, Adjudications and Clearance Processes at a Glance," webpage, undated-d. As of July 7, 2023:
https://www.dcsa.mil/mc/pv/mbi/gicp/

Defense Counterintelligence Security Agency, "Security Assurances for Cleared Individuals and Facilities," webpage, undated-e. As of July 11, 2023:
https://www.dcsa.mil/mc/isd/int/security/

DeSouza, Eros R., Eric D. Wesselmann, and Dan Ispas, "Workplace Discrimination Against Sexual Minorities: Subtle and Not-So-Subtle," *Canadian Journal of Administrative Science/ Canadiennenadienne des scien'es de l'administration*, Vol. 34, No. 2, 2017.

Director of Central Intelligence Directive No. 1/14 and Annex A Adjudication Guidelines, "Minimum Personnel Security Standards and Procedures Governing Eligibility for Access to Sensitive Compartmented Information," Central Intelligence Agency, May 13, 1976.

DistillerSR, homepage, undated. As of July 7, 2023:
https://www.distillersr.com/

EARN—*See* Employer Assistance and Resource Network on Disability Inclusion.

Emory, Allison Dwyer, "Protective State Policies and the Employment of Fathers with Criminal Records," *Social Problems*, 2021.

Employer Assistance and Resource Network on Disability Inclusion, "Neurodiversity in the Workplace," webpage, undated. As of August 16, 2023:
https://askearn.org/page/neurodiversity-in-the-workplace

England, Paula, "The Gender Revolution: Uneven and Stalled," *Gender & Society*, Vol. 24, No. 2, 2010.

Entman, Robert M., "Framing: Toward Clarification of a Fractured Paradigm," Journal of Communication, Vol. 43, No. 4, 1993.

Executive Order 13869, "Transferring Responsibility for Background Investigations to the Department of Defense," Executive Office of the President, April 24, 2019.

Executive Order 13985, "Advancing Racial Equity and Support for Underserved Communities Through the Federal Government," Executive Office of the President, January 2021.

Executive Order 14035, "Diversity, Equity, Inclusion, and Accessibility in the Federal Workforce," Executive Office of the President, June 2021.

Farrell, Brenda, S., *Personnel Security Clearances: Additional Actions Needed to Ensure Quality, Address Timeliness, and Reduce Investigation Backlog*, U.S. Government Accountability Office, GAO-18-29, 2017.

Farrell, Brenda, S., *Personnel Security Clearances: Additional Actions Needed to Implement Key Reforms and Improve Timely Processing of Investigations*, U.S. Government Accountability Office, GAO-18-431T, March 2018.

Feagin, Joe R., *Living with Racism: The Black Middle-Class Experience*, Beacon Press, 1995.

Ford, Erica, and Hiren Shukla, "How to Engage Neurodivergent Talent in the Government Workforce," GovLoop, April 1, 2022.

Fordham University, School of Law, *Cutting-Edge Developments in Neuroscience and Law*, February 25, 2020.

GAO—*See* U.S. Government Accountability Office.

Garon, Thea, "Young Adults' Credit Trajectories Vary Widely by Race and Ethnicity," Urban Institute, August 22, 2022.

Heckenberg, Suzanne Wilson, and Alison Berman, "Promote Neurodiversity in the Intelligence Community," ClearanceJobs, October 6, 2021.

Heilman, Madeline E., "Description and Prescription: How Gender Stereotypes Prevent Women's Ascent Up the Organizational Ladder," *Journal of Social Issues*, Vol. 57, No. 4, 2001.

Heilman, Madeline E., "Gender Stereotypes and Workplace Bias," *Research in Organizational Behavior*, Vol. 32, 2012.

Heilman, Madeline E., and Tyler G. Okimoto, "Why Are Women Penalized for Success at Male Tasks?: The Implied Communality Deficit," *Journal of Applied Psychology*, Vol. 92, No. 1, 2007.

Henle, Christine A., Gwenith G. Fisher, Jean McCarthy, Mark A. Prince, Victoria P. Mattingly, and Rebecca L. Clancy, "Eldercare and Childcare: How Does Caregiving Responsibility Affect Job Discrimination?" *Journal of Business and Psychology*, Vol. 35, 2020.

Hess, Kathleen P., "Investigation of Nonverbal Discrimination Against Women in Simulated Initial Job Interviews," *Journal of Applied Social Psychology*, Vol. 43, No. 3, 2013.

Institute for Women's Policy Research, "Gender and Racial Wage Gaps Persist as the Economy Recovers," fact sheet, September 2022.

Khan, Maria Hameed, Mirit K. Grabarski, Muhammad Ali, and Stephen Buckmaster, "Insights into Creating and Managing an Inclusive Neurodiverse Workplace for Positive Outcomes: A Multistaged Theoretical Framework," *Group & Organization Management*, October 2022.

Kochhar, Rakesh, and Anthony Cilluffo, *Income Inequality in the U.S. Is Rising Most Rapidly Among Asians*, Pew Research Center, 2018.

Krzeminska, Anna, Robert D. Austin, Susanne M. Bruyère, and Darren Hedley, "The Advantages and Challenges of Neurodiversity Employment in Organizations," *Journal of Management & Organization*, Vol. 25, No. 4, 2019.

Kyzer, Lindy, "What Is the Whole Person Concept?" ClearanceJobs, September 4, 2019.

Lamont, Michèle, Graziella Moraes Silva, Jessica Welburn, Joshua Guetzkow, Nissim Mizrachi, Hanna Herzog, and Elisa Reis, *Getting Respect: Responding to Stigma and Discrimination in the United States, Brazil, and Israel*, Princeton University Press, November 2016.

Lewis, Tené T., Frances M. Yang, Elizabeth A. Jacobs, and George Fitchett, "Racial/Ethnic Differences in Responses to the Everyday Discrimination Scale: A Differential Item Functioning Analysis," *American Journal of Epidemiology*, Vol. 175, No. 5, 2012.

Ligor, Douglas C., Shawn D. Bushway, Maria McCollester, Richard H. Donohue, Devon Hill, Marylou Gilbert, Heather Gomez-Bendaña, Daniel Kim, Annie Brothers, Melissa Bauman, Barbara Bicksler, Rick Penn-Kraus, and Stephanie J. Walsh, *Criminal History Record Information Sharing with the Defense Counterintelligence and Security Agency: Education and Training Materials for State, Local, Tribal, and Territorial Partners*, RAND Corporation, RR-A846-1, 2022. As of June 22, 2023:
https://www.rand.org/pubs/research_reports/RRA846-1.html

Loiacono, Eleanor T., and Huimin Ren, "Building a Neurodiverse High-Tech Workforce," *MIS Quarterly Executive*, Vol. 17, No. 4, 2018.

Manson, Katrina, "Neurodiversity Emerges as a Skill in Artificial Intelligence Work," Bloomberg, October 18, 2022.

Mallory, Christy, Andrew R. Flores, and Brad Sears, "Workplace Discrimination and Harassment Against LGBT State & Local Government Employees," Williams Institute, 2021.

Mong, Sherry N., and Vincent J. Roscigno, "African American Men and the Experience of Employment Discrimination," *Qualitative Sociology*, Vol. 33, No. 1, 2010.

Morris, Meredith Ringel, Andrew Begel, and Ben Wiedermann, "Understanding the Challenges Faced by Neurodiverse Software Engineering Employees: Towards a More Inclusive and Productive Technical Workforce," *Proceedings of the 17th International ACM SIGACCESS Conference on Computers & Accessibility*, 2015.

National Geospatial Intelligence Agency, "NGA Launches Neurodiversity Pilot," press release, January 13, 2021.

National Institute on Minority Health and Health Disparities, "Structural Racism and Discrimination," webpage, undated. As of July 7, 2023:
https://www.nimhd.nih.gov/resources/understanding-health-disparities/srd.html

National Security Memorandum 3, "Memorandum on Revitalizing America's Foreign Policy and National Security Workforce, Institutions, and Partnerships," Executive Office of the President, February 2021.

NGA—*See* National Geospatial Intelligence Agency.

Ogrysko, Nicole, "Biden Calls for Agency Ideas to Win the Race for National Security Talent," Federal News Network, February 5, 2021.

OPM—*See* U.S. Office of Personnel Management.

Pager, Devah, "The Mark of a Criminal Record," *American Journal of Sociology*, Vol. 108, No. 5, 2003.

Pager, Devah, "The Use of Field Experiments for Studies of Employment Discrimination: Contributions, Critiques, and Directions for the Future," *Annals of the American Academy of Political and Social Science*, Vol. 609, No. 1, 2007.

Pager, Devah, and Hana Shepherd, "The Sociology of Discrimination: Racial Discrimination in Employment, Housing, Credit, and Consumer Markets," *Annual Review of Sociology*, Vol. 34, August 2008.

Pager, Devah, Bart Bonikowski, and Bruce Western, "Discrimination in a Low-Wage Labor Market: A Field Experiment," *American Sociological Review*, Vol. 74, No. 5, 2009.

Paré, Guy, and Spyros Kitsiou, "Chapter 9: Methods for Literature Review," in F. Lau and C. Kuziemsky, eds., *Handbook of eHealth Evaluation: An Evidence-Based Approach*, National Library of Medicine, February 2017.

Piquado, Tepring, Sina Beaghley, Lisa Pelled Colabella, and Nahom M. Beyene, *Assessing the Potential for Racial Bias in the Security Clearance Process*, RAND Corporation, RR-A1201-1-v2, 2022. As of June 21, 2023:
https://www.rand.org/pubs/research_reports/RRA1201-1-v2.html

Posard, Marek N., Emily Ellinger, Jamie Ryan, and Richard S. Girven, *Updating Personnel Vetting and Security Clearance Guidelines for Future Generations*, RAND Corporation, RR-A757-1, 2021. As of June 22, 2023:
https://www.rand.org/pubs/research_reports/RRA757-1.html

Posard, Marek N., Christian Johnson, Julia L. Melin, Emily Ellinger, and Hilary Reininger, *Looking for Lies: An Exploratory Analysis for Automated Detection of Deception*, RAND Corporation, RR-A873-1, 2022. As of June 30, 2023:
https://www.rand.org/pubs/research_reports/RRA873-1.html

Praslova, Ludmila N., "Autism Doesn't Hold People Back at Work. Discrimination Does," *Harvard Business Review*, December 13, 2021.

Quillian, Lincoln, John J. Lee, and Mariana Oliver, "Evidence from Field Experiments in Hiring Shows Substantial Additional Racial Discrimination After the Callback," *Social Forces*, Vol. 99, No. 2, December 2020.

Ragins, Belle Rose, Romila Singh, and John M. Cornwell, "Making the Invisible Visible: Fear and Disclosure of Sexual Orientation at Work," *Journal of Applied Psychology*, Vol. 92, No. 4, 2007.

Sabia, Joseph J., Thanh Tam Nguyen, Taylor Mackay, and Dhaval Dave, "The Unintended Effects of Ban-the-Box Laws on Crime," *Journal of Law and Economics*, Vol. 64, No. 4, 2021.

Sears, Brad, Christy Mallory, Andrew R. Flores, and Kerith J. Conron, *LGBT People's Experiences of Workplace Discrimination and Harassment*, Williams Institute, September 2021.

Security, Suitability, and Credentialing Performance Accountability Council, "Trusted Workforce 2.0 Implementation Strategy: Mission, Mobility, Insight," April 2022.

Security, Suitability, and Credentialing Performance Accountability Council, "Trusted Workforce 2.0 Implementation Strategy: Mission, Mobility, Insight," March 2023.

Sluzki, Carlos E., "Transformations: A Blueprint for Narrative Changes in Therapy," *Family Process*, Vol. 31, No. 3, 1992.

Sumner, Kenneth E., and Theresa J. Brown, "Neurodiversity and Human Resource Management: Employer Challenges for Applicants and Employees with Learning Disabilities," *Psychologist-Manager Journal*, Vol. 18, 2015.

Thomas, Teresa, "Pilot Increases Neurodiversity in Government," MITRE, April 2, 2021.

USAJOBS, homepage, undated. As of August 16, 2023:
https://www.usajobs.gov/

U.S. Department of Labor, "Earnings Disparities by Race and Ethnicity," webpage, undated. As of July 6, 2023:
https://www.dol.gov/agencies/ofccp/about/data/earnings/race-and-ethnicity

U.S. Department of Labor, Office of Disability Employment Policy, "Tapping the Power of Neurodiversity in the Workplace," *Business Sense Newsletter*, December 2021. As of July 6, 2023: https://www.dol.gov/agencies/odep/publications/business-sense/2021/december

U.S. Office of the Director of National Intelligence, *Security Executive Agent Directive 4: National Security Adjudicative Guidelines (SEAD-4)*, National Counterintelligence and Security Center, June 8, 2017.

U.S. Office of Personnel Management, "Standard Form 86, Questionnaire for National Security Positions," last updated November 2016.

U.S. Office of Personnel Management, "Standard Form 85, Questionnaire for Non-Sensitive Positions," last updated December 2017a.

U.S. Office of Personnel Management, "Standard Form 85P, Questionnaire for Public Trust Positions," last updated December 2017b.

U.S. Office of Personnel Management, "Standard Form 85P-S, Supplemental Questionnaire for Selected Positions," last updated December 2017c.

U.S. Office of Personnel Management, "Notice of Submission for a New Information Collection Common Form: Personnel Vetting Questionnaire," *Federal Register*, Vol. 87, No. 225, November 23, 2022.

Volpone, Sabrina D., Scott Tonidandel, Derek R. Avery, and Safiya Castel, "Exploring the Use of Credit Scores in Selection Processes: Beware of Adverse Impact," *Journal of Business and Psychology*, Vol. 30, 2015.

Vuolo, Mike, Sarah Lageson, and Christopher Uggen, "Criminal Record Questions in the Era of 'Ban the Box,'" *Criminology & Public Policy*, Vol. 16, No. 1, 2017.

Wakefield, Sara, and Christopher Uggen, "Incarceration and Stratification," *Annual Review of Sociology*, Vol. 36, 2010.

Weinbaum, Cortney, Omair Khan, Teresa D. Thomas, and Bradley D. Stein, *Neurodiversity and National Security: How to Tackle National Security Challenges with a Wider Range of Cognitive Talents*, RAND Corporation, RR-A1875-1, 2023. As of June 30, 2023: https://www.rand.org/pubs/research_reports/RRA1875-1.html

White, Michael, *Maps of Narrative Practice*, W. W. Norton & Company, 2007.

Williams, David R., Yan Yu, James S. Jackson, and Norman B. Anderson, "Racial Differences in Physical and Mental Health: Socio-Economic Status, Stress and Discrimination," *Journal of Health Psychology*, Vol. 2, No. 3, 1997.

Wilson, Valerie, and William Darity, Jr., "Understanding Black-White Disparities in Labor Market Outcomes Requires Models that Account for Persistent Discrimination and Unequal Bargaining Power," Economic Policy Center, March 25, 2022.

Wingfield, Adia Harvey, and Koji Chavez, "Getting In, Getting Hired, Getting Sideways Looks: Organizational Hierarchy and Perceptions of Racial Discrimination," *American Sociological Review*, Vol. 85, No. 1, 2020.

Winslade, John, "Tracing Lines of Flight: Implications of the Work of Gilles Deleuze for Narrative Practice," *Family Process*, Vol. 48, No. 3, 2009.

Winslade, John, and Gerald D. Monk, *Narrative Mediation: A New Approach to Conflict Resolution*, John Wiley & Sons, 2000.